MAMMALS OF LAKE TAHOE

MAMMALS OF LAKE TAHOE *by*

Robert T. Orr

CURATOR OF BIRDS AND MAMMALS
CALIFORNIA ACADEMY OF SCIENCES

ILLUSTRATED BY

GEORGE AND PATRITIA MATTSON

CALIFORNIA ACADEMY OF SCIENCES

San Francisco, California

1949

PRINTED IN THE UNITED STATES OF AMERICA
BY THE HOWELL-NORTH PRESS, BERKELEY

15835

To the memory of
my friend and associate
JAMES MOFFITT

CONTENTS

LIST OF ILLUSTRATIONS

INTRODUCTION

Lake Tahoe, because of its size, natural beauty, and situation in the high central Sierra Nevada, is world famous like many of the other scenic wonders that nature has created in western North America. Year after year thousands of visitors from near and far come to enjoy this great expanse of mountain water and the rugged peaks that surround it.

To gain a full appreciation of such a region, however, requires an understanding of all the factors that contribute to make it so fascinating to the human mind — the sky, the earth, the water, the living creatures both plant and animal, and its history before and since the coming of man. George Wharton James in his delightful book *The Lake of the Sky* has attempted to describe these many and varied phases of this beautiful country.

The present work is for the benefit of those who would delve somewhat deeper into the habits of the fifty-three kinds of native mammals that either live here at present or have been so recorded in the past. Although designed primarily as a field guide for those who come to Lake Tahoe, this book may prove equally useful in other regions since many of the animals included range more or less extensively over the Sierra Nevada as well as other mountainous areas in the West.

The descriptions given for each species do not necessarily apply to the species as a whole. Many of the mammals occurring about Lake Tahoe are geographically variable forms exhibiting different bodily proportions and coloration in other parts of their ranges. An attempt has been made, therefore, to describe each kind, briefly yet adequately, as it appears in this region. Proper, vernacular names of mammalian species are capitalized throughout the text (for example, Yellow Pine Chipmunk) while common names used in the generic sense (for example, chipmunk) are not capitalized.

1

For those who wish to see many of the mammals described here an account is given of the local occurrence of each kind as well as its general distribution over the world. Space limitation in a work of this sort necessarily precludes extensive life history accounts but an attempt has been made to sketch some of the more salient features relating to the natural history of the species considered. A short historical summary of Lake Tahoe and a description of the region, especially the more conspicious botanical features, are included as well as a glossary for the benefit of many who may be unfamiliar with the few technical terms that had to be used. Those wishing to further their knowledge of this area and the mammals that inhabit it will find a selected list of references.

The major illustrations were prepared by George and Patritia Mattson of San Francisco. I am especially grateful to them for their careful and painstaking work which is outstanding, both as regards the accuracy of the animals portrayed and artistic result. The tracks were sketched by Grace Crowe Irving who also assisted in many other ways in the preparation of this work. I am indebted to Mary Lou Perry for many valuable suggestions and for her assistance in the critical reading of the manuscript and proofs.

HISTORY OF LAKE TAHOE

Advancing civilization has produced great changes in our country within the past few hundred years but, until recent times, the West has been the last to feel its effects. New York, Philadelphia and Washington were thriving industrial, scientific and political centers, respectively, when John C. Fremont and his party of explorers had the privilege, on February 14, 1844, of being the first white men to view Lake Tahoe. Since that memorable day, barely more than a century ago, this now world-famous place of scenic beauty has witnessed many changes, brought about by the hand of man.

Fremont first referred to this body of water as "mountain lake." Later, in the account of his expedition to Oregon and California, he named it Lake Bonpland, in honor of Aimé Bonpland the eminent French botanist who accompanied the explorer Baron Alexander von Humboldt. In 1853 the name was officially changed to Lake Bigler, in honor of the third Governor of California, John Bigler.

It was William Henry Knight, with the strong support of John S. Hittell, editor of the *Alta California,* a San Francisco newspaper, and Dr. Henry DeGroot, a writer for the *Evening Bulletin,* who succeeded in having the name of Lake Bigler changed to Tahoe, the native Indian name. This appeared on the first general map of the Pacific States, published in 1862 by the Bancroft Publishing House of San Francisco.

Other names were suggested and considerable opposition arose for a time against acceptance of the name Tahoe. Well known personalities entered the conflict, including Mark Twain who humorously derided the word in *The Innocents Abroad,* saying that it meant "grasshopper soup." Today few persons are even aware that any name other than Tahoe, meaning "high water" or "big water" in the Washoe Indian dialect, was ever applied to this lake.

3

At the time the white men came to this region it was used as a summer hunting ground by the Washoe Indians. Members of this tribe wintered farther east in the Carson and Washoe valleys but as the warmer season approached they migrated westward to the Tahoe shores where fish, game, nuts, berries, roots and other edibles were present in abundance.

With the discovery of gold in the West, especially the Comstock Lode in 1859 which resulted in the birth of Virginia City, a thriving lumber industry developed about the lake, and the towns of Glenbrook, Tahoe City and Incline came into existence. Untold millions of board feet of lumber were removed during the next few decades but this business finally waned before the turn of the century. Meanwhile, the region had built up a reputation for its scenic beauty and especially for the fine hunting and fishing it afforded. Its recreational value came more and more into prominence when a railroad connection with the main transcontinental line at Truckee was established in 1900. The replacement of the stage coach by the automobile and the construction of fine modern highways have now opened this beautiful sierran area to vast numbers of people.

I recall my first childhood trip to the high Sierra Nevada, which included a visit to Lake Tahoe and the Yosemite Valley. Such journeys then seemed arduous but exciting. Two full and hectic days were entailed in the drive from San Francisco to Lake Tahoe. Here I had my first glimpse of a chipmunk and Belding Ground Squirrel. Today Lake Tahoe is within a few hours' driving distance of many cities and towns in California and Nevada. Its shores are dotted with summer homes and some of its resorts beckon to visitors the year around. Many, preferring closer contact with nature, avail themselves of the fine camp grounds maintained by the United States Forest Service and the California State Park system.

DESCRIPTION OF THE TAHOE REGION

In ages past, geologists tell us, the first Sierra Nevada was elevated to great heights. Long and continued erosion then gradually wore these rugged spires down to smooth and gently rolling slopes. Later, a second period of uplift came along and the present mountain chain was formed. Many changes, however, were to occur before this great range attained its present appearance. In the central part, with which we are here concerned, a split took place along the main summit, resulting in two crests. The newly formed valley between these crests then sank and became even more pronounced. Later on extensive lava flows cut this valley in two. The northern one we presently know as Sierra Valley and the southern one constitutes the basin in which Lake Tahoe now exists.

These newly formed mountains were steep and rugged, marked by sharp angles and V-shaped valleys. It was not until the late Ice Age, when vast glaciers covered most of this terrain, that its present form began to appear. These huge ice fields moved slowly down the slopes, carving, gouging, and planing the rouch surfaces into smooth basins such as we see here today. When the Ice Age ended these basins caught the water from the melting snow and formed the many lakes that now are scattered throughout this region. The great Lake Valley no longer was filled with a frozen mass but contained the second largest body of water in the world above the 6000-foot level.

Today it stands out like an enormous gem, its color changing locally by the hour each day, from pale blue to emerald, from amethyst to the deepest purple. Sixteen hundred and forty-five feet deep, it defies the coldest winters to freeze its surface completely.

Though the summits of the loftiest peaks, like Mt. Rose, Pyramid and Freel peaks, rise above timber line and may retain patches of snow the year around, no true glaciers now exist here. The granitic slopes of the mountains surrounding the lake are, for the

5

most part, clothed with loose coniferous forests whose presence and particular composition are important factors influencing the distribution of many kinds of mammals.

At lower elevations Jeffrey pine, sugar pine, white fir and incense cedar are the most conspicuous trees. The first two species mentioned are especially valuable for their timber and so, in years past, were heavily logged off in numerous places about the lake. There are still, however, many untouched stands to be seen, and second growths from fifty to seventy-five years in age have in some places nearly obliterated the scar of the woodman's axe. Green manzanita, tobacco brush, snow-brush, wild currant, huckleberry oak and chinquapin are among the more common kinds of plants comprising the forest undercover. On certain treeless slopes these shrubs form a dense chaparral which one can penetrate only with great difficulty. In warmer, more arid situations, particularly on the Nevada side of the lake, many plants from the Great Basin desert to the eastward have made an invasion. Sagebrush, rabbit brush, desert mahogany and antelope brush are not uncommon.

The creeks are lined with mountain alder, willows of several different kinds, quaking aspen, American dogwood, Sierra maple, mountain ash, bitter cherry, and service berry, as well as many other trees, shrubs, and herbaceous plants.

At higher elevations the character of the forest changes. Trees that were so common near lake level are gone and have been replaced by other species. White pine, lodgepole pine and red fir predominate, and near timber line mountain hemlocks stand tall and slender with gently drooping heads. Alpine meadows of brilliant green and patches of native heather are common at these heights.

Occasionally at the upper limits of tree growth, on wind-swept ridges and desolate slopes, a few stunted white bark pines or western junipers, gnarled and prostrate, cling to the rocky surface as though in constant fear of being torn from their moorings.

—

Geological formations and the presence or absence of various kinds of plants are frequently found to be important factors controlling the distribution of many kinds of mammals. Some species, however, show far greater environmental restriction than others. The American Badger ranges from below sea level, as in Death Valley, to above timber line in the high Sierra Nevada, its presence depending not so much on climate or plant life directly, as upon the availability of rodents for food. The Pika or Cony, in western United States, is an animal almost entirely confined to the higher mountains and there it is found only in rock slides. In this instance home sites of a very particular type and perhaps climate are the limiting factors, because the plants upon which Pikas feed are by no means confined to the immediate vicinity of talus slopes. Other species, such as the Red Squirrel, occur only in coniferous forests. A simple knowledge of the geology and the principal botanical features of a region, therefore, may serve as a considerable aid to one who is seeking information regarding its animal life.

THE CLASSIFICATION OF MAMMALS

The living things of the earth are divided into two great Kingdoms, one comprising the plants, including everything from minute bacteria to the highest types of flowering plants, and the other including all forms of animal life from one-celled creatures to man. Each of these Kingdoms in turn is divided into a number of great subdivisions called Phyla. The first Phylum in the Animal Kingdom is the Phylum Protozoa which contains the unicellular organisms, and the highest Phylum is called the Chordata. The latter includes all those animals that at some time in their life cycle possess a dorsal strengthening rod called a notochord, which, in a sense, is the forerunner of the vertebral column. The chordates are divided into several Sub-Phyla one of which is the Sub-Phylum Vertebrata. The latter includes all animals possessing a vertebral column of one sort or another.

The living vertebrates are divided into six or seven Classes, the lowest being the Class Cyclostomata which includes primitive, jawless, fish-like creatures, such as the Lamprey Eels. The highest is the Class Mammalia which contains the most highly developed forms of organic life.

Mammalia or mammals, as they are commonly called, differ from other vertebrates such as birds, reptiles, amphibians, or fishes, in a number of structural features. One of the chief differences is, as their name mammal implies, the fact that they possess mammary glands, whose secretions provide food for their young. Another mammalian feature is the possession of hair. Although there are certain mammals, such as whales, in which the hair is so greatly reduced that it may be present only during early development or else is represented by but a few bristles in the adult, most mammals have a well-developed coat of hair covering their bodies. Many other structural characters might be mentioned, including the presence of a muscular diaphragm, three bones or auditory

8

ossicles in the middle ear, and the fact that the lower jaw is composed of a single pair of bones, the dentaries. These and a large number of other mammalian features, however, are apparent only to the anatomist and cannot be discerned by a cursory observation of the living animal.

Just as Kingdoms are divided into smaller groups called Phyla and Phyla divided into Classes so also are Classes divided into smaller categories called Orders. There are a number of living Orders of mammals in the world but we shall concern ourselves only with those occurring in the Lake Tahoe region. Here we find six different mammalian Orders represented, if we exclude man (Order Primates) even though the Washoe Indians were native to the area before the arrival of the white man. The six Orders are the Insectivora, Chiroptera, Carnivora, Rodentia, Lagomorpha and Artiodactyla.

The Order Insectivora is represented in this area by the Broadfooted Mole and four species of long-tailed shrews. Our insectivores are all small, the mole being largest, and all have pointed snouts and a relatively large number of teeth with well defined cusps. The mole possesses 44 teeth and the long-tailed shrews have 32. All of them have fur that is short, soft, almost velvety in the mole, and various shades of dark gray or brownish-gray in color. Both moles and shrews are short-legged and possess minute eyes, which in the former are almost rudimentary.

The Order Chiroptera includes the bats, five species of which have been recorded so far from around Lake Tahoe. Bats are the only true flying mammals. They possess this ability because of the great elongation of the bones of their fingers and palms between which are stretched double membranes connecting with the sides of the body and the hind legs. This is correlated with a great development of the chest and shoulder muscles. The ears are almost always relatively large, and in some species are enormous in proportion to body size. All of our bats are insectivorous and nocturnal or crepuscular.

The Order Carnivora is perhaps better known than most of the others. It contains the typical flesh-eating animals, although many species are actually quite omnivorous. Included in this group are the bears, raccoons, weasels, mink and skunks. At least 15 species of carnivores have been recorded about Lake Tahoe within recent years, although some, because of excessive hunting and trapping, are now exceedingly rare. The teeth of members of the Carnivora are usually well adapted for cutting and tearing flesh and the canines usually project a considerable distance beyond the incisors and premolars. Our most valuable fur-bearers belong to this Order.

The Order Rodentia contains the great majority of the small mammals of the world. None of the members of this Order attains a large size, the beaver and porcupine being the largest native rodents in North America. All are characterized by the presence of but two incisor teeth in the upper jaw and two in the lower. These teeth are conspicuously large, have enamel only on their front surfaces and are separated from the molariform teeth by a large space or diastema. Twenty-two species of rodents have been recorded from the Lake Tahoe basin. These include various kinds of mice, the wood rat, squirrels, chipmunks, the pocket gopher and others. Some are nocturnal, some diurnal, some live almost entirely beneath the ground, others on the ground or in trees, some are semi-aquatic and one species, the Northern Flying Squirrel, can even glide through the air. Structural characters, therefore, rather than habits or adaptations, serve best to define the group.

The Order Lagomorpha includes the hares, rabbits and pikas. In certain respects they show relationship to the rodents and some students of mammalian classification include the two groups in the same Order. There are certain differences, however, by which the lagomorphs can always be distinguished. Their upper jaw always shows the presence of four incisors, the second pair being very small and situated directly behind the first pair, instead of being lateral to them as in the case of other mammals possessing four upper incisors. The incisor teeth possess enamel on their posterior as well as anterior surfaces. The tail in all forms is very much shortened.

The Artiodactyla are the even-toed, hoofed mammals, such as sheep, cattle, goats, pigs, deer and many other familiar animals. Quite a few species have been domesticated and a large number are highly sought after for food and sport. The functional toes never number more than four and frequently two of these are so reduced in size that only the remaining two on each foot are used in running or walking. Practically all members of the Order are herbivorous and most of them are of large size. Deer are the only native artiodactyls living in the Lake Tahoe region at present. It is probable, however, that in early days the Big Horn or Mountain Sheep once occurred on the higher peaks, but the nearest known recorded locality for the occurrence of this species within historic times is the vicinity of Donner Pass.

For convenience in classification and to indicate closer relationships Orders are divided into Families. A list of the mammalian Families occurring in this region will be found in the Table of Contents. Families in turn are divided into Genera and, finally, Genera into Species.

KEY TO THE MAMMALS OF LAKE TAHOE

In the following key all of the species of mammals considered in this book are arranged according to the presently accepted natural system of classification to indicate, in so far as is possible, their relationships to one another. This is the same order that is followed in the text. Except for occasional references to teeth, all of the characters used are external. Some of these will be apparent at a glance, while others will necessitate a careful examination of the animal in hand.

Keys, for the most part, are artificial since they generally attempt to separate complex things, such as different kinds of animals or plants, on the basis of one or, at most, a very few obvious characters. Not infrequently the most obvious differences between related kinds are the least important or, as is often the case, closely related species are distinguished from one another by a number of slight differences that are discernible only upon a careful and detailed examination. An artificial key, therefore, may on occasions be misleading or may even fail in its purpose. In general, however, it is of some assistance to the beginner and even though it may not enable one to distinguish all closely related forms, at least it will indicate the group to which a particular species belongs. More accurate identification can then be made by carefully reading the descriptions and habits of the various members of such a group to determine those most applicable to the subject in question.

1 External ears lacking_____Broad-footed Mole, p. 17
1' External ears present.
  2 Eyes very minute; snout long and pointed.
    3 Total length less than 5 inches.
      4 Tail sharply bicolored_____Trowbridge Shrew, p. 19
      4' Tail not sharply bicolored.
        5 Total length usually less than $4\frac{3}{8}$ inches; tail length usually less than $1\frac{3}{4}$ inches_____Vagrant Shrew, p. 20
        5' Total length usually more than $4\frac{3}{4}$ inches; tail length usually more than $1\frac{3}{4}$ inches_____Dusky Shrew, p. 20
    3' Total length greater than 5 inches_____Water Shrew, p. 21
  2' Eyes not very minute; snout not unusually long and pointed.
    6 Fore limbs modified for flight.
      7 Wingspread less than 11 inches; general color some shade of brown.
      8 Ears about $\frac{1}{2}$ inch long; fur dark brown.

      9 Fur on back with glossy sheen_____Little Brown Bat, p. 23

      9' Fur on back generally dull brown_____Yuma Bat, p. 23

    8' Ears about ¾ inch long; fur pale golden brown

    _____Long-eared Bat, p. 24

  7' Wingspread generally 11 inches or more.

    10 Smaller (wingspread about 11 inches); color, blackish, with some hairs tipped with silvery-white_____Silvery-haired Bat, p. 24

    10' Larger (wingspread about 14 inches); color rich brown_____

    _____Big Brown Bat, p. 25

6' Fore limbs not modified for true flight.

  11 Canine teeth proportionately large and projecting beyond incisors and premolars.

    12 Hind foot possessing 5 toes.

      13 Size large; adults often attaining a total length of 5 feet_____

      _____Black Bear, p. 29

      13' Size medium or small.

        14 Tail banded with alternating light and dark rings_____

        _____ Raccoon, p. 33

        14' Tail not noticeably banded.

          15 General color (in summer) some shade of brown; no conspicuous white stripes on head or upper parts of body.

          16 Toes not webbed.

            17 Underpart of body white, yellow or with orange-buff patches; or, if not, tail longer than 12 inches.

            18 Tail bushy.

              19 Tail 6 to 8 inches long_____Pine Marten, p. 35

              19' Tail 14 to 17 inches long_____Fisher, p. 38

            18' Tail slender and pencil-like with terminal third or fourth black.

              20 Tail from 2½ to 3½ inches in length_____

              _____Short-tailed Weasel, p. 40

              20' Tail from 4½ to 6¼ inches in length_____

              _____Long-tailed Weasel, p. 41

            17' Underpart of body brown or with white patch or patches on neck, chest or belly; tail less than 12 inches long_____American Mink, p. 44

          16' Toes webbed_____River Otter, p. 46

        15' General color black and white or silvery-gray; conspicuous white stripes present either on head or upper parts of body.

        21 Body not flattened in appearance; color, black and white.

22 Four to six narrow, longitudinal bands of white on back and sides of body_____Spotted Skunk, p. 48

22' Two longitudinal white bands on back_____Striped Skunk, p. 50

21' Bodily form, appearing broad and flat; general color silvery-gray__ _____American Badger, p. 53

12' Hind foot possessing only 4 functional toes.

23 Facial region long and dog-like; claws not retractile.

24 Total length usually less than 3½ feet; tip of tail white; general color of upper parts rusty red_____Red Fox, p. 55

24' Total length about 4 feet; tip of tail usually black; general color of upper parts grayish-buffy_____Coyote, p. 58

23' Facial region short and cat-like; claws retractile.

25 Total length 6 to 8 feet; tail length, 2 feet or more_____ _____Mountain Lion, p. 61

25' Total length, less than 3 feet; tail 5 to 7 inches in length_____ _____ Bobcat, p. 64

11' Canine teeth, if present, not projecting beyond incisors and premolars.

26 Feet not provided with hooves; more than two functional toes present on each foot; size medium or small.

27 No more than 2 incisor teeth in upper jaw.

28 Body lacking quills or spines.

29 Tail not noticeably longer than head and body.

30 Tail not so small as to be inconspicuous.

31 Tail not compressed laterally.

32 Total length, about 2 feet_____ _____Yellow-bellied Marmot, p. 66

32' Total length, less than 20 inches.

33 Squirrel- or chipmunk-like in appearance.

34 No loose folds of skin connecting fore- and hind legs on either side of body.

35 Tail short, equal to less than ¼ total length_____ _____Belding Ground Squirrel, p. 68

35' Tail longer, equal to ⅓ or more of total length.

36 Total length, at least 16 inches; fur of back dappled_____ _____California Ground Squirrel, p. 70

36' Total length, never over 14 inches; fur of back never dappled.

37 One or more pairs of white stripes present on back or sides.

38 No obvious white stripes on head, above and below eyes; no dark stripe down center of back_____ _____Golden-mantled Ground Squirrel, p. 73

38′ Obvious white stripes on head, above and below eyes; dark stripe down center of back.

39 Length of head and body usually less than 4¾ inches; fur on underside of body usually buffy_____Yellow Pine Chipmunk, p. 76

39′ Length of head and body usually more than 4¾ inches; fur on underside of body generally white or grayish.

40 Length of head and body less than 5 inches_____
_____Lodgepole Chipmunk, p. 77

40′ Length of head and body more than 5 inches.

41 Ears proportionately short and rounded, less than ¾ inch in length; light spot behind each ear grayish-white_____
_____ Townsend Chipmunk, p. 77

41′ Ears proportionately long and pointed, about ¾ inch in length; light spot behind each ear clear white_____
_____Long-eared Chipmunk, p. 78

37′ White stripes lacking from back and sides_____Red Squirrel, p. 81

34′ Loose folds of skin connecting fore- and hind legs on either side of body_____Northern Flying Squirrel, p. 84

33′ Appearance not squirrel- or chipmunk-like.

42 External, fur-lined cheek pouches present_____
_____Mountain Pocket Gopher, p. 87

42′ External, fur-lined cheek pouches absent.

43 Ears conspicuous, never buried in fur.

44 Total length never exceeding 9 inches; tail sparsely haired.

45 Total length, never exceeding 7¼ inches_____
_____Deer Mouse, p. 90

45′ Total length, over 7½ inches.

46 Dorsal tail stripe broad; length of ear less than length of hind foot_____Brush Mouse, p. 91

46′ Dorsal tail stripe narrow; length of ear greater than length of hind foot_____True White-footed Mouse, p. 91

44′ Total length, over 12 inches; tail bushy_____
_____Bushy-tailed Wood Rat, p. 94

43′ Ears nearly buried in fur.

47 Color pale gray above; tail length decidedly less than ½ length of head and body_____Gray Lemming Mouse, p. 96

47′ Color dark gray; tail length varying from slightly less to more than ½ length of head and body.

48 Length of tail usually less than ⅓ total length; tail not decidedly bicolored_____Montane Meadow Mouse, p. 96

48′ Length of tail usually more than ⅓ total length; tail decidedly bicolored............Long-tailed Meadow Mouse, p. 97

31′ Tail laterally compressed and conspicuously scaled.............
.... Muskrat, p. 100

30′ Tail so small as to be hardly visible......Mountain Beaver, p. 102

29′ Tail longer than combined length of head and body...............
.... Big Jumping Mouse, p. 105

28′ Body covered with conspicuous quills or spines...................
....North American Porcupine, p. 107

27′ Four incisor teeth in upper jaw; second pair small and located directly behind first pair.

49 Ears small and rounded; tail hardly discernible...............Pika, p. 110

49′ Ears of moderate or large size; tail proportionately short but conspicuous.

50 Size, large; hind foot over 4¼ inches in length.

51 Hind foot usually more than 5¾ inches in length; tail almost entirely white, both above and below.......................
....White-tailed Jack Rabbit, p. 112

51′ Hind foot usually less than 5¾ inches in length; tail (in summer) never white.

52 Total length not more than 16 inches; tail, about 1½ inches long.. Snowshoe Rabbit, p. 113

52′ Total length not less than 20 inches; tail, about 3½ inches long..Black-tailed Jack Rabbit, p. 113

50′ Size, small; hind foot less than 4¼ inches in length...................
.... Nuttall Cottontail, p. 116

26′ Feet provided with hooves; no more than two functional toes on each foot; size large....................Mule or Black-tailed Deer, p. 119

ORDER INSECTIVORA — Insect-eating Mammals

FAMILY TALPIDAE — Moles

P&G MATTSON

BROAD-FOOTED MOLE
Scapanus latimanus

Description — *Total length, 6 to 7 inches; tail length, 1¼ to 1½ inches. Body, stocky, with nose long and snout-like. Tail, short and thick. Eyes and ears, hardly visible externally. Front legs, short and lateral in position. Front feet, extremely broad and flat, with proportionately large claws. Fur, short, soft and silky, silvery-gray in color, both above and below. Tail, sparsely covered with coarse hairs. Whiskers, inconspicuous.

General Distribution — From southern Oregon, south through California and parts of western Nevada, to northern Lower California, exclusive of the Mohave and Colorado Desert areas.

Local Distribution — Of common occurrence in meadows and forests, wherever the soil is moist and not too rocky.

---

*For definition of *total length* and *tail length* see Glossary.

17

Habits — Moles are the most strictly subterranean mammals present in North America. Their bodies are streamlined and their fur is very soft, both adaptations to an existence beneath the surface of the ground. Rarely are they exposed to the light of day; consequently their minute eyes, which are almost hidden by fur, are probably of little functional value. The most striking structural features characterizing these animals, however, are the short, sturdy front limbs with their broad palms and strong claws. These forelegs, which extend out laterally from the body instead of being directed downward as in most land mammals, permit the mole to push the earth aside as it drives its body through the ground, especially when foraging an inch or so beneath the surface. The elevated ridges, so often seen where the soil is moist, are the results of such activity. The long, fleshy snout is very sensitive and as it passes through the earth it ferrets out insects, worms and other types of animal food. Although these tunnels just below the surface of the ground may be used more than once, they are of a relatively transitory nature.

Permanent burrow systems are constructed by moles a foot or more beneath the ground, as a result of excavation. The soil from these deeper passageways cannot simply be pushed up all along, as is possible near the surface. Instead we find that at various points along the burrow system there are vertical shafts leading to the surface. The excavated soil from below is pushed up these shafts to the outside. As a result, mounds, somewhat resembling pocket gopher mounds, are formed. They may be distinguished from the latter by the fact that the earth is in small clods, rather than finely broken up. Furthermore, since the excavating shafts of the mole are nearly vertical, instead of being broadly inclined as in the pocket gopher, the mouth of the shaft is directly below the center of the mound instead of being to one side.

Although moles may do damage to gardens, such injury is incidental so far as they are concerned since they are non-vegetarians.

Roots may be broken or exposed to air as a result of sub-surface foraging by these animals for small invertebrates in the soil.

Moles are active the year around as the snow in winter does not conflict with their activities in the warmer earth beneath. They are most widespread in late spring and early summer, however, when much of the ground is still damp. As the warmer season comes and the surface moisture is restricted, so likewise is the available habitat for moles reduced.

The young are probably born in March or April in this region. The usual number in a litter is four, although it may vary from two to five. They are naked and helpless at time of birth.

FAMILY SORICIDAE — Shrews

P & G MATTSON

TROWBRIDGE SHREW
Sorex trowbridgii

Description — Total length, about 4½ inches; tail length, 2 inches. Nose, long and pointed. Tail, slender and scantily haired. Eyes minute and external ears small and partly hidden in the surrounding fur. Front and hind legs and feet normally proportioned, in relation to body size. Fur of medium length, soft and dense. Color, grayish-brown above, only slightly paler below. Tail, sharply bicolored. Whiskers small but distinct.

General Distribution — From extreme southwestern British Columbia, south through western Washington and Oregon to Santa Barbara County, California, along the coast; south through the Sierra Nevada to the Kaweah River, Tulare County, California; barely entering Nevada in the Lake Tahoe region and along the Truckee River.

Local Distribution — Present in small numbers near streams and lakeshores, as well as in marshy situations.

VAGRANT SHREW
Sorex vagrans

Description — Total length, about 4 inches; tail length, 1½ inches. Similar in general appearance to the Trowbridge Shrew but smaller, with tail uniformly grayish-brown instead of bi-colored, and underparts of body decidedly paler than back.

General Distribution — South through much of the mountainous portions of western North America, from British Columbia to southern Mexico; in California, south along the coast to the San Francisco Bay region and in the Sierra Nevada south to Mono County; in the northern half of Nevada, principally in the higher mountains.

Local Distribution — Similar to the preceding species.

DUSKY SHREW
Sorex obscurus

Description — Except for slightly larger size and longer tail this species is hardly distinguishable, on the basis of external characters alone, from the Vagrant Shrew.

General Distribution — From central Alaska south in western North America to New Mexico; in California, throughout most of the higher Sierra Nevada, also the San Bernardino and San Gabriel mountains; in Nevada, only in the Lake Tahoe region.

Local Distribution — Similar to that of the Trowbridge and Vagrant shrews, but more apt to be found at higher elevations.

WATER SHREW

Sorex palustris

Description — Total length, about 6 inches; tail length, 3 inches. Similar in general bodily shape to the three other species of shrews occurring in the Tahoe region, but decidedly larger and with feet more heavily haired along margins. Color of upper parts, a grizzled grayish-black; underside of body, pale grayish-white. Tail, distinctly bicolored.

General Distribution — Rather widely distributed over northern North America, from southern Alaska east to Nova Scotia, and south, locally, in western United States to Arizona; in California, in the northern Coast Ranges and south in the Sierra Nevada to the vicinity of Mt. Whitney; in Nevada, principally in the mountains in the northern half of the state.

Local Distribution — Restricted to the vicinity of rather rapidly flowing streams.

HABITS

The smallest species of mammals in the world are shrews and the smallest mammal in the Lake Tahoe region is the Vagrant Shrew. Because of their general similarity in habits the four species of long-tailed shrews occurring here are considered collectively.

The Water Shrew because of its semi-aquatic habits is rarely, if ever, found far from flowing streams, but the other three species often live beneath logs on moist forest floors, around springs and seepages and in marshes and damp meadows. However, as they are nocturnal, of small size and inconspicuous, the average person rarely has the opportunity to observe these tiny animals.

Like their relatives, the moles, shrews live on animal food such as insects and worms. Given the opportunity they will eat small mammals, including mice and even other shrews. The voracious appetite and savageness of these little animals is well illustrated in an account described by the late C. Hart Merriam of three shrews that were placed together in a container: "Almost immediately they commenced fighting, and in a few minutes one was slaughtered and eaten by the other two. Before night one of these killed and ate its only surviving companion, and its abdomen was much distended by the meal. Hence in less than eight hours one of these tiny wild beasts had attacked, overcome, and ravenously consumed two [*sic*] of its own species, each as large as itself."

Unlike moles, shrews do most of their foraging on the surface of the ground, often beneath leaf litter. Both their eyes and ears are functional, but it is likely that their sense of smell is relied upon mostly in securing food. So far as known, they are active all winter beneath the snow.

The Water Shrews differ somewhat from the other species in their adaptations to semi-aquatic life. They are expert swimmers and are also capable of floating, diving, walking on the bottom of a stream and, what is even more remarkable, walking on the surface of the water. This latter feat has been witnessed by a number of persons and seems possible partly as a result of the presence of a prominent fringe of hairs about the margins of the feet which thereby increases the amount of surface.

Because of their propensity for water these shrews are sometimes captured by trout. Members of this species, as well as the other kinds of shrews, are occasionally taken by predatory birds and mammals. Generally speaking, however, shrews are not much sought after as food by other animals. It is possible they possess certain body glands that produce an obnoxious odor or taste. Certain species are known to possess poison glands in the mouth.

Relatively little is known of the breeding habits of shrews, but from the data at hand it may be concluded that most of our species bear their young in late spring and summer. The number of young per litter varies from 3 to 9, with 6 being about the average.

ORDER CHIROPTERA — Flying Mammals

FAMILY VESPERTILIONIDAE — Common Bats

P & G MATTSON

LITTLE BROWN BAT
Myotis lucifugus

Description — A small bat with a wingspread of about 10 inches. Total length, averaging 3¼ inches; tail length, 1½ inches. Color, dark brown above, paler and more buffy on underparts. Hairs on back, possessing a glossy sheen. Ears, about ½ inch in length and blackish in color like flight membranes.

General Distribution — From the northern limits of tree growth in Alaska, east to Labrador, south throughout most of the United States, and possibly to southern Mexico.

Local Distribution — Practically throughout the forested parts of the Lake Tahoe area.

YUMA BAT
Myotis yumanensis

Description — Very similar to the Little Brown Bat, but most readily distinguished from members of that species by the dull color of the hairs on the back, and, in this region, by the brownish rather than blackish ears.

General Distribution — Western North America, from southern British Columbia south to central Mexico.

Local Distribution — Forested or brushy areas at lower elevations.

LONG-EARED BAT

Myotis evotis

Description — Slightly larger than the Little Brown Bat and Yuma Bat, but with proportionately very long ears which average about ¾ inch in length. Color of fur on back, pale golden brown. Tips of hairs on underparts of body whitish or very pale buff.

General Distribution — Western North America, from southern British Columbia east to North Dakota, and south to central Mexico.

Local Distribution — Probably of rare occurrence in forested areas at lower elevations. Only two specimens have been recorded from the Lake Tahoe region and both were taken on Mt. Tallac.

SILVERY-HAIRED BAT

Lasionycteris noctivagans

Description — Somewhat larger than any of the preceding species of bats, with a wingspread of about 11 inches. Total length, 3¾ to 4 inches; tail length, 1½ inches. Fur, blackish, with some of the hairs tipped with silvery-white. Ears, averaging slightly less than ½ inch in length and black like the flight membranes.

General Distribution — Forested parts of much of northern North America, from the Atlantic to the Pacific, north of Mexico.

Local Distribution — Probably of regular occurrence in the forested parts of the Lake Tahoe region, at least during the summer months. So far as known, however, but a single specimen has been recorded from this area. This was secured at Bijou.

Big Brown Bat

Eptesicus fuscus

Description — Superficially resembling bats of the genus *Myotis* but much larger, with a wingspread of nearly 14 inches. Total length, averaging about 4½ inches; tail length, 1¾ to 2 inches. Color above, rich brown, slightly paler below. Ears about ½ inch in length and blackish like flight membranes.

General Distribution — From southern Canada to Central America, with closely allied forms occurring in the West Indies.

Local Distribution — Fairly common, except at high elevations, throughout the region.

Habits

Five species of bats belonging to three different genera have been recorded so far from the Lake Tahoe region, and it is likely that several additional species which have heretofore been overlooked will be discovered here in the future. Three of the species belong to the genus *Myotis* which is one of the most widely distributed mammalian genera in the world, its members occurring within the limits of tree growth in both the Eastern and Western Hemispheres and on most of the larger islands. The great majority of the small bats seen flying in the evening in the Lake Tahoe region belong to this group. Of the three species of *Myotis* occurring here the Little Brown Bat is undoubtedly the most common and widest ranging form, being found from lake level to timber line.

The Silvery-haired Bat, on the other hand, belongs to a unique American genus, represented by a single species, while the Big Brown Bat has many close relatives in Asia, Australia, Africa and Madagascar.

Bats in general are intriguing to human beings, having long been associated in our folklore with witches and superstitions. Actually our North American species are very useful little animals and play an important part in the control of certain insect populations. They are harmless, will not try to get tangled in your hair, and some, if kept in captivity, become friendly within a short time.

Bats are the only mammals possessing the true power of flight. This has been accomplished through extreme elongation of the bones of the hand and the development of a thin double membrane connecting the fingers and palm, as well as the arm, with the hind leg and tail. To produce the powerful wing strokes necessary to maintain the body in the air bats have developed remarkably large chest muscles, resembling in many respects those of birds, and, as with flying birds, the breast bone of most bats possesses a keel to give increased surface for muscle attachment.

Although some kinds of bats live on fruit, others on blood and some even on fish which they catch themselves, most of our western North American species are insect eaters, securing their food generally on the wing. The latter habit accounts largely for the erratic type of flight in which bats usually indulge, especially in the early evening when they seem rarely to fly more than a few feet without twisting, turning, dropping or performing some other unpredictable aërial gyration.

Because of their remarkable ability to secure flying insects at night bats have often been credited with an extra sense. The eyes of our North American species show no unusual development, although they probably function quite well. Experiments performed on bats which have had their eyes completely covered, however, have shown that they can fly and avoid hitting minute objects, such as fine wires suspended in a room, just as efficiently under these circumstances as they can with their vision unimpaired. Interference with the auditory apparatus of bats, on the other hand, has a definitely adverse effect upon their normally uncanny power to avoid hitting obstacles in flight.

Recent investigations indicate that bats make use of reflected sound waves. This same principle of sonar is employed in navigation to determine the depth of water and in certain respects resembles radar except that the latter relies upon the reflection of electro-magnetic waves. In each instance the speed of the impulse is known and, from the time required for it to be reflected back to its point of origin, the distance of the reflecting surface can be computed.

The reflected sounds or echoes which bats hear are made by the animals themselves. They are of such high frequency as to be above the upper limits of human audibility and are called super-sonic sounds, although they can be detected by a delicate instru-ment known as a supersonic analyser.

In flight bats may emit these sounds as often as fifty times a second if they are close to objects. The frequency of utterance decreases the farther they are from the point of reflection since more time is required for the echo to return. It is claimed by one group of investigators that to avoid confusion of transmission with reception there are small muscles in the ears of bats which momentarily contract and cut off the reception of sound when a directive note is uttered so that only the echo is received. The ability to emit supersonic sounds and to control their rate of utterance, plus a very highly developed ear, therefore, appears to explain how bats avoid hitting objects while flying at night and also secure food on the wing. No doubt they also can readily detect the faint buzzing sounds produced by flying insects. Bats have very well developed sensory hairs and membranes which, likewise, are believed to function as receptors for vibrations set up in the air by insects close by.

Some species of bats are colonial while others are solitary for the most part. The Little Brown Bat, the Yuma Bat and the Big Brown Bat are definitely gregarious in their habits, large numbers often living together in caves. Around Lake Tahoe, as in many other places, these bats have taken advantage of man-made habi-tations and thereby increased their available homesites by occupy-ing attics. The Long-eared Bat and the Silvery-haired Bat are believed to be solitary species, at least during most of the year.

Dense foliage in trees, crevices in bark and in rocks, rather than caves, serve to hide them during the daytime.

Although only the thumb of the fore appendage of North American bats possesses a claw, the toes of the hind legs have well developed claws which serve admirably to suspend these animals upside down when they are resting or sleeping. This is the posture frequently assumed at such times. Most of the bats of the Lake Tahoe region become active about dusk and may be seen silhouetted against the sky before it becomes too dark. Members of the three species of *Myotis* are most apt to be seen flying about small forest clearings or among trees, from medium heights to within a few feet of the ground. Their flight is rapid and erratic. Big Brown Bats tend to fly higher, often 50 feet or more above the ground and their flight is slower, while the Silvery-haired Bat shows a decided preference for the vicinity of water, frequently flying low over streams or lakeshores in search of insects.

Generally, where it is cold in winter, cave-dwelling species of bats become dormant while tree-inhabiting species usually migrate to regions where the climate is milder. The Silvery-haired Bat is one of those species whose migrations are fairly well known in eastern United States. Little is known, however, regarding the seasonal movements of bats in the West. When snow mantles the higher Sierra Nevada in winter bats are no longer seen flying about in the evening, but whether they have migrated to lower levels or are merely in hibernation, remains to be determined in the case of each species.

In this region bats bear their young chiefly during the months of June and July. At this season, even among colonial species there is often a segregation of the sexes, the males keeping away from the females and young. The females of the species considered here usually have one young a year, although occasionally there may be two. The babies cling to the mother's breast and fur by means of their mouths and proportionately large feet and thumbs during the first few days after birth. They even remain attached when she flies about foraging. After their weight begins to increase noticeably, however, they are left at home in the roosting place until they become old enough to fly of their own accord.

Bats, in general, have relatively few enemies, as is indicated by the small number of young born annually. Occasionally, however, they are captured by hawks and owls, as well as carnivorous mammals. There are also a number of records of bats being eaten by large trout. This has happened when bats have accidentally dropped into the water or have been flying low over the surface of streams and lakes.

ORDER CARNIVORA — Flesh-eating Mammals

FAMILY URSIDAE — Bears

BLACK BEAR
Ursus americanus

Description — Size, very large, with adult males sometimes attaining a length of over 5 feet. Tail, very short, usually less than 6 inches long. Body, stout, with proportionately short, sturdy legs. Toes provided with long, strong nails. Hind foot sometimes measuring as much as 10½ inches in length. Fur, moderately long, coarse and dense, varying in color from light brown to black.

General Distribution — From the northern limits of tree growth in North America, south to northern Mexico; in California, formerly south in the Coast Ranges almost to San Francisco Bay and south throughout the Sierra Nevada to the Tehachapi Mountains; in Nevada, only in the Lake Tahoe region.

Local Distribution — Although not often seen, except occasionally about the larger garbage dumps, where they are attracted by food, Black Bears are present in small numbers in the Lake Tahoe basin, principally below the 8000-foot level.

Habits — So far as known there is no historic record of Grizzly Bears occurring in the Lake Tahoe region. Although these huge animals were once common in the lowlands and foothills of California, they apparently shunned the higher parts as well as the east-central slopes of the Sierra Nevada where Black Bears, even to this day, are not uncommon.

While Black Bears, in general, do not attain the great size of old Grizzlies, they may weigh as much as 500 pounds. Most Black Bears, however, do not weigh much over 300 pounds. A female of this size was caught by Steve Craig along Blackwood Creek on November 1, 1926. Another female, taken 3 miles up Ward Creek by James Moffitt on November 9, 1926, weighed only 115 pounds.

The Black Bear is a naturally shy animal and, except where it has been tamed by man, is rarely seen in the wild. Unlike the Grizzly which, before it became extinct in California, dwelt principally in the chaparral belt below the 2000-foot level, the Black Bear is a forest inhabitant. Consequently, it rarely comes into conflict with the activities of man. Occasionally a larder will be plundered but this is usually the result of carelessness on the part of man, for which the bear can hardly be blamed.

The name Black Bear for this animal is an unfortunate one and has led to a great deal of confusion. Within the range of this species in California and western Nevada the majority of Black Bears are not black but various shades of brown or cinnamon. These are not different varieties of bears but mere color variations which may occur in the same litter.

Bears, somewhat like human beings, are omnivorous, eating both plant and animal food. In the spring of the year bulbs, leaves, grass and insects may be taken along with mice, young birds, and squirrels. Honey is always desirable, when it can be obtained. In the autumn, nuts, berries, grubs and other fattening foods are eaten in preparation for the lean winter season.

Black Bears are agile tree climbers, learning this trick when they are quite young. Mother bears will immediately chase their cubs up a tree whenever there is a threat of danger. So called "bear trees" are more often seen in the woods than the bears themselves. These are trees in which bears seem regularly to scratch their claws and sink their teeth. Apparently this is done when they are standing on their hind legs as the marks are usually well up on the trunk. Aspens and incense cedars in this region are most often selected for this purpose. Although not definitely known, it is suspected that these bear trees are somewhat similar in function to the scent posts of certain other animals.

Black Bears are reputed to hibernate in the winter but they do not actually hibernate in the true sense, as do ground squirrels or marmots. Their body temperature does not become noticeably lowered nor is their rate of respiration markedly slowed down. Furthermore, they can be aroused from their dens in caves or hollow trees on almost a moment's notice, if necessary. This winter sleep usually extends from early December until late March or April in this region. It is probable that where food is available some Black Bears around Lake Tahoe may be active all winter.

The young are born during the winter period. The usual number of young in a litter is 2 or 3, although extremes of 1 and 4 have been recorded. Black Bears are extremely small at birth, in proportion to the size of the adults, reportedly weighing between

one-half and three-fourths of a pound. Since Black Bears are solitary animals except during the brief mating period in the summer,
the duties of rearing the young are entirely the responsibility of
the female. The young remain in or close to the den in which they
are born until late spring, then accompany their mother for the
following year. Adult females appear to breed only every other
year.

Generally speaking Black Bears are harmless animals. Normally in the wild they will detect your approach and be gone long
before you have opportunity to obtain even a glimpse of them.
Under certain circumstances, however, such as when cornered,
wounded, or when their young are in danger, they may become
formidable opponents. Black Bears are frequently maligned as
deer and stock killers but the accusation is usually false. Certain
individuals at times may become killers, but more often than not
Mountain Lions, Coyotes or Bobcats are the culprits and the bear
has merely come along and cleaned up the remains, leaving his
conspicuous and tell-tale tracks which appear as *prima facie* evidence of guilt and lead to a hasty and false conviction.

FAMILY PROCYONIDAE — Raccoons

RACCOON
Procyon lotor

Description — Total length, 2½ to 3 feet; tail length, 12 to 14 inches; ear, 2 to 2½ inches long. General color, grayish-brown with numerous black-tipped hairs on back. Face marked by a conspicuous black mask. Tail, bushy and circled by about six black bands. Average weight, about 13 pounds, but individuals have been known to weigh as much as 30 pounds.

General Distribution — Throughout most of North America from southern Canada south, probably to Central America. Of common occurrence in California, except in the higher Sierra Nevada and the south-eastern desert areas; less common in Nevada, being restricted to the extreme northern and western portions of the state and to the vicinity of the Colorado River and its tributaries in the southern part.

Local Distribution — Very uncommon in the Lake Tahoe region, where a few individuals have been known to occur, principally on the Nevada side.

Habits — Raccoons are for the most part inhabitants of the lowlands and foothills where they occur along creeks and rivers, even in marshes and on the seacoast. Few are found at high elevations in the mountains. The author has rarely observed signs of Raccoons about Lake Tahoe although their tracks are not uncommon several miles down the Truckee River from its source. Two specimens were secured at Marlette Lake by Dr. E. Raymond Hall and recorded in his book on the *Mammals of Nevada*. This, incidentally, is the highest locality in the Sierra Nevada at which this species is known to have been taken. On June 22, 1947, however, the writer and his wife observed the distinct footprints of a Raccoon in mud next to a small pool formed by melting snow, one mile southeast of the Velma Lakes at an elevation of 8500 feet.

Raccoons are nocturnal animals, spending the daylight hours in hollow trees, dens in rock piles, holes in banks or beneath root stumps. Evidence of their nightly activity is most often shown by the tracks that they leave in the mud along streams or lake shores. These footprints are very distinct and readily recognizable, presenting a hand-like appearance, with five long distinct toes and the palm print in the impression.

Members of this species are usually solitary, but on occasions a number of individuals may occupy the same hole or den. They are not in any sense aquatic animals but do show a definite preference for the vicinity of ponds and streams, probably because their food is most readily obtainable in these places.

Raccoons, somewhat like bears, are omnivorous, subsisting on a wide variety of foods. Small rodents, birds, eggs, frogs, fish, shellfish, fruits, berries and acorns are all commonly eaten when obtainable. Raccoons are active all the year around, but when the weather is very cold in winter they may hole up for days at a time, until climatic conditions become more favorable.

The young are generally born in April or May, the number in a litter varying from 3 to 7 and averaging about 4.

Raccoons at times may kill poultry and do damage to crops, particularly orchards, but in general they are of considerable value to man. They function as scavengers, play an important part in keeping small rodent populations in check, furnish pleasure to sportsmen and are one of our more important fur-bearers. In some years the total value of Raccoon pelts secured by trappers in California has exceeded that of pelts of any other single species of fur-bearing mammal. They are of considerably less importance in Nevada, due to their very restricted distribution in that state.

FAMILY MUSTELIDAE — Weasels, Skunks, etc.

PINE MARTEN
Martes caurina

Description — About the size of a small house cat, but with body slender and weasel-like. Total length, nearly 2 feet; tail length, 6 to 8 inches. Color, brown, except for one or more patches of fur on underside of neck and chest, which may vary from pale buff to deep orange-yellow. Fur, rich, soft, and of medium length. Tail, quite bushy, with hairs near tip darker brown than those of the body in general. Ears, broadly rounded, and from 1 to 1¾ inches long. Legs, fairly short in proportion to body size. Soles of feet well furred, with claws slender and sharp.

General Distribution — Of wide occurrence over the forested parts of northern North America[1]; south along the Pacific coast to Tulare County in the Sierra Nevada; barely entering western Nevada in the vicinity of Lake Tahoe.

Local Distribution — Not uncommon at higher elevations, in or close to coniferous forests; sometimes found inhabiting rocky slopes.

Habits — The Pine Marten is one of the most valuable fur-bearing mammals occurring in the Lake Tahoe region. It has been recorded by trappers from most of the higher mountains about the lake but is probably most common on the western side, above 7000 feet. Rarely do these animals come down to lake level, although on one occasion tracks were seen in the snow about one-fourth of a mile up McKinneys Creek. Members of this species exhibit a distinct preference for talus slopes during the summer months. Here they seek small mammals, such as marmots, Deer Mice, Bushy-tailed Wood Rats and Pikas. In the winter, when the rock slides are buried deep beneath the snow, Pine Martens most often frequent red fir forests. They are skillful at climbing trees and nimble at jumping from branch to branch. At this season of the year they live to a large extent on Red Squirrels, flying squirrels, and even certain woodpeckers.

Because of the Pine Marten's natural wariness of man and preference for the higher parts of the mountains, few persons ever have the opportunity of seeing it. Tracks in the snow in winter, however, shed a great deal of light on the habits of these animals. Although usually solitary, they appear sometimes to travel in small packs, or at least a number of individuals use the same trail within a period of a few hours. The distance travelled by a single individual during a night may amount to as much as 10 or 15 miles. While these trails appear somewhat erratic, they do actually follow

---

[1]Although several species of martens, with more or less complementary ranges, are presently recognized as occurring in North America, it is possible that future study will ultimately reveal them to be merely geographic variants of a single species. The range given above includes all American forms of marten.

a rather definite course over a hunting territory. Each marten or group of martens, appears to have several such hunting territories. After one has been used for a few nights it will be deserted for a week or two during which time other circuits will be travelled. When hunting for squirrels in the winter along ridges clothed with red fir martens may travel for long distances through the trees, without ever descending into the snow.

While principally nocturnal, the activities of members of this species, at least during the winter months, do not appear to be confined entirely to the night. On one occasion in late November, 1941, the author observed a marten diligently following a Red Squirrel in the middle of the afternoon on a high ridge near the Sonora Pass. So intent was it in the pursuit of its prey that it failed to see the observer who was no more than ten yards away. Between November 4 and 20, 1926, the late Robert M. Watson, veteran guide at Lake Tahoe, and the late James Moffitt, secured 8 Pine Martens in traps in the Velma Lakes region. The last one taken was caught between 8 a.m. and 1 p.m.

There is no indication that martens hibernate in winter, although they do seem to stay in their dens during extremely stormy weather. These dens often consist of modified Red Squirrel or woodpecker holes in dead fir trees; sometimes they are located in rock piles.

The young are reportedly born in April and attain maturity by the following autumn. The number in a litter appears to vary from 1 to 4.

In California the Pine Marten is considered as one of the most valuable fur-bearers, although marten pelts from this state do not command as high a price as do those from farther north.

According to those who have trapped marten for many years and are familiar with their habits, the principal enemies of these animals now, at least in this region, are Horned Owls and Golden Eagles. No doubt they are occasionally captured by larger species of carnivorous mammals.

FISHER

Martes pennanti

Description — Total length, 2½ to 3½ feet; tail length, 14 to 17 inches. Somewhat resembling a marten in general appearance but much larger and possessing a proportionately longer tail. Color, grayish-brown, becoming more grayish on head and nearly black down the middle of the back. Feet, nose and tail, blackish. Fur, moderately long and soft. Tail, bushy.

Geographical Distribution — Formerly, from southeastern Alaska and northwestern Canada east to Nova Scotia; south through the Appalachian Mountains; south in the Rocky Mountains to Wyoming; south along the mountains of the Pacific coast to the southern Sierra Nevada. Present range greatly restricted throughout, but especially in eastern North America.

Local Distribution — Extremely rare visitant, if occurring at all at present.

Habits — The Fisher is now considered to be a rare mammal in California and, so far as known, has never been recorded in

Nevada. It is listed here with the mammals of Lake Tahoe on the basis of references to its former occurrence in this region made by George Wharton James (1915, p. 311) and on the basis of tracks noted in the snow back of Tahoe Tavern on November 21, 1926 by the late James Moffitt and Robert M. Watson.

The name Fisher is strikingly inadequate for members of this species which are to a large extent arboreal and rarely partake of fish. Probably the native Indian name of Pekan, if generally accepted, would be more suitable, but vernacular names, once established, are difficult to change. In appearance the Fisher resembles an over-sized marten in many respects, but is even more agile than its smaller relative which at times it pursues and catches for food.

Members of this species, like mink and marten, are solitary, for the most part, and have extensive territories covering a good many square miles. Over these territories they have fairly definite routes which are regularly travelled. Several weeks, however, may be required to complete the circuit. Their dens, according to trappers familiar with the habits of these animals, are generally in holes in trees or cavities in fallen logs and, like those of many others of the weasel family, smell heavily of their owner's scent.

Fishers generally inhabit forested country, occurring at lower altitudes in the mountains than Pine Marten. There are many localities, however, where the two species occur together.

Fishers are active principally at night but on occasions they have been observed foraging in the daytime. The speed with which they can travel from tree to tree through a forest without coming to the ground, while hunting or when pursued, has been remarked upon by many. Grinnell, Dixon and Linsdale (1937, p. 224) cite an observation made by a veteran trapper, William H. Parkinson, in the southern Sierra Nevada, wherein an individual of this species travelled for one-quarter of a mile through the tree tops at a speed nearly as fast as the observer could run.

Fishers are active all winter, often securing small mammals beneath the surface of the snow. Their food varies seasonally and is, of course, dependent upon the presence or local abundance of various kinds of small animals. It includes Gray Squirrels, Red Squirrels, mice, wood rats, chipmunks, pocket gophers, marmots, Mountain Beavers and even porcupines. Birds are occasionally eaten but do not usually constitute a major item of food.

Very little is known of the breeding habits of these animals but the young are reported to be born in May and a litter is said to contain from 2 to 4 babies. The adults have few enemies, apart from man, because of their great strength and agility, but Mountain Lions occasionally prey upon them.

The Fisher is our most valuable fur-bearing mammal but in the West, as throughout most of its range, its numbers have been greatly reduced in the last few decades through persistent trapping. In California, Fisher pelts bring the highest price of any native fur-bearer, more than double those of marten which hold second place in this regard. The average price paid to trappers for Fisher pelts taken in California during the winter of 1940-41 was $39.62 and the highest price for any one skin was $51.75. In 1920 the average price in this same state for these pelts was $67.33. As can be judged from the foregoing figures, the monetary incentive to trap these animals is so great that the species is doomed to extinction in all but our larger National Parks, unless it is afforded strict protection before it is too late.

SHORT-TAILED WEASEL
Mustela erminea

Description — Total length, varying from about 7 to 12 inches with the males considerably larger than the females; tail length, 2½ to 3½ inches. Body, proportionately long and slender. In summer, general color above, nearly chocolate brown. Underside of body, white or creamy white. Tail, slender, with proximal two-thirds about the same color as back, both above and below, and distal third black. In winter, color entirely white, except for distal third of tail which is black.

General Distribution — Europe, northern Asia and northern North America; south in higher Sierra Nevada of California to the Yosemite region; in Nevada, occurring on some of the higher mountains, at least in the northern half of the state.

Local Distribution — Of relatively rare occurrence in the higher parts of the Lake Tahoe region.

P & G MATTSON

Long-tailed Weasel
Mustela frenata

Description — Similar in general proportions to the Short-tailed Weasel, but considerably larger, and with a relatively longer tail. Total length, 12½ to 18 inches; tail length, 4½ to 6¼ inches. Color in summer, brown above and yellow below, except for chin which is whitish. Tail, brown, except for tip which is black. In winter, entirely white, except for tip of tail which is black.

General Distribution — North, Central and South America, from southern Canada south to Venezuela, Colombia, Ecuador and

Peru. Widely distributed over California and Nevada except for extreme desert areas.

Local Distribution — Likely to be found almost anywhere from lake level to timber line, both in forested and open country.

HABITS

Two widely ranging kinds of weasels occur in the Lake Tahoe region. One of these, the smaller, short-tailed species, is more northern in distribution and is found in both the Old and New World, while the Long-tailed Weasel is restricted to the New World but occurs in both the northern and southern hemispheres.

In the higher mountains of California and Nevada, as in many other parts of their ranges where the winters are cold and there is an abundance of snow, individuals of both species become white in winter. This is accomplished by a molt in the late fall, at which time the brown summer coat is replaced by a white one. In the spring the white coat is shed and again a brown pelage is assumed. This white coloration in winter is distinctly to the advantage of these animals in the snow-covered environment, protecting them from their enemies and also making it easier for them to stalk other small mammals upon which they depend largely for food. The white winter coat of the weasel is really "ermine," although in the fur trade the name is generally restricted to the pelts of Old World species.

Weasels are the smallest carnivores in the Lake Tahoe area, in fact the smallest living carnivore in the world today is believed to be the Least Weasel of the North. Despite their diminutive size, however, they are truly ferocious little animals and are greatly feared by many other small mammals.

In the Lake Tahoe region weasels are apt to be found almost anywhere, although the Short-tailed Weasel occurs only at higher elevations. Individuals of both species, however, may live in densely forested areas, open meadows, streamsides or rock slides. The type of environment does not appear to be so important as is the presence of small rodents in numbers. The burrows of other animals, especially pocket gophers, are often occupied by weasels although at times they may live among rocks, in hollow logs or even in buildings.

Although weasels are active principally at night, it is not unusual to see them about in the daytime. One afternoon in early September the author watched a Long-tailed Weasel actively moving around in a rock slide above the Velma Lakes near Dick's Peak. It travelled over the smaller rocks and under the larger ones. Pikas were numerous in this same slide and it was suspected that the weasel lived on these animals. On another occasion, in late June, a Long-tailed Weasel was seen in the afternoon running across the ground in a lodgepole pine forest, several miles northeast of Tahoe City. It was carrying what appeared to be a freshly caught chipmunk in its mouth.

Pocket gophers, various kinds of mice, chipmunks and squirrels as well as Bushy-tailed Wood Rats, Pikas and certain other small mammals are all suitable food for weasels in this region. It is likely that on certain occasions small birds may be taken but they constitute a very minor part of the diet of weasels. In killing their prey it is customary for them to seize the victim by the back of the neck or the base of the skull and then sever the spinal column with their sharp teeth. They seem to show preference for the blood rather than the flesh of animals that they kill. When food is plentiful weasels appear at times to slaughter for the pleasure of it. This occurs on occasions when an individual gets into a poultry yard.

Young weasels are probably born during May and June in this region. The number in a litter appears usually to range from 3 to 6. So far as known, the young are cared for entirely by the mother, the male parent, as in many other carnivores, not participating in this phase of the family life.

Little is known of the enemies of weasels but Ernest Thompson Seton suggests that this animal is its own worst enemy. Individuals are so incompatible in many instances that fatal fights often result. Perhaps this explains why weasels never seem to become too abundant in any region.

American Mink
Mustela vison

Description — Total length, about 18 to 24 inches; tail length, usually 6 to 8 inches. General bodily proportions, somewhat resembling a weasel's, but considerably larger, stockier, and with relatively smaller ears and shorter tail. Tail, bushier than that of a weasel, and tapering rather than giving appearance of uniform diameter from base to tip. General color, dark brown, becoming blackish toward tip of tail. A patch or patches of white are frequently present on the underside of the neck, chest or belly.

General Distribution — Throughout much of North America from northern Alaska, east to Labrador and south to Florida; throughout most of northern and central California as far south as Fresno and Inyo counties; limited in Nevada to the northeastern and extreme west-central parts.

Local Distribution — Known to occur along the Truckee River and, locally, about the shores of Lake Tahoe as well as some of the larger creeks draining into the lake.

Habits — Like the Pine Marten the mink is one of our valuable fur-bearing mammals. The fur of the latter, however, differs from that of the marten in that it is coarse in texture and has more of a luster. Like other members of the weasel family, mink have scent glands, the secretions from which possess an obnoxious odor.

Since mink are semi-aquatic the presence of permanent water appears to be a rather critical factor governing the distribution of the species. They do not care for small streams that dry up during the warm summer period because a large proportion of the animals upon which they depend for food also require water. Mink frequently live in piles of drift wood. Sometimes they occupy holes in banks or even dens in rocks. They are swift and skillful swimmers and at times catch much of their food in the water.

A wide variety of animal food is consumed by mink, including crayfish, mussels, fish, frogs, snakes, small mammals, especially rodents, birds and eggs. Dead birds and other edible refuse washed ashore or otherwise found are also readily eaten. Mink do not have the reputation of being killers like the weasels, but frequently they catch more food than they can eat. This is often cached and returned to for later consumption, provided other animals have not plundered the larder in the meantime.

Mink, as a rule, are rather solitary creatures. Their tracks are more often seen than are the animals themselves, since they are largely nocturnal and have somewhat of a distaste for humans. These footprints are frequently observed along the muddy banks of streams where mink have recently foraged.

Not much is known of the breeding habits of mink but the young are reported to be born in April or May and cared for by the mother. There are usually from 4 to 7 in a litter.

Mink have relatively few natural enemies but the Horned Owl is said to capture them on occasions.

River Otter
Lutra canadensis

Description — Total length, about 3½ feet; tail length, approximately 18 inches. Body slender and weasel-like, with tail thick at base and tapering distally. Fur, moderately short and dense, dark glossy brown in color except for lighter area extending from mouth to chest. Legs, proportionately short; toes, webbed. Whiskers, rather conspicuous.

General Distribution — Most of North America, from northern Alaska south to the Mexican border. Formerly absent in the United States only from certain desert regions in the southwest, though present range much reduced through trapping. Occurs throughout much of the northern half of California and locally along the larger streams and lakes in northern Nevada as well as along the Colorado River in both states.

Local Distribution — Of rare occurrence in the Tahoe region, having been found in recent years only at Marlette Lake.

Habits — Although River Otters occur widely over North America they can hardly be considered as numerous anywhere. Their fur is valuable but, at least in much of western United States, their population has been so reduced that they cannot be classed as important fur-bearers at present.

River Otters, as their name implies, are found principally along larger water courses and lakes. Their bodies are long and streamlined, their ears very small and their toes webbed. All these features are adaptations to a semi-aquatic life, for these animals are expert swimmers and depend upon this ability for the capture of much of their food. The long muscular tail, which tapers from a very thick base, is a great aid in propelling the body through water. At such times it is thrashed laterally, in an undulating manner, in rhythm with a similar motion on the part of the hind quarters.

These animals may be active both at night and during the daytime. Frequently they spend hours sunning themselves on a bank. They are known for their playfulness and seem to derive much pleasure from coasting down mud slides from the tops of steep river banks into the water. They are also especially fond of rolling over and over on the ground or in grass at certain spots selected for this activity. Their voice is loud and shrill, having a rather bird-like quality.

River Otters live primarily upon fish, most of which they capture themselves by rapidly pursuing these creatures through the water. However, other kinds of animal food, especially crayfish, are eaten in quantity when available.

Otters frequently make use of dens, some of which appear to have been originally constructed by other animals. They are usually located under steep banks situated next to water. Here the young are born and reared until able to follow their mother on hunting excursions. The female bears a single litter a year, generally in April or May. The number of young in a litter varies from 1 to 4 and is said to average about 3.

It is not known whether the male parent remains with the female and young but it seems likely that he at least lives close by and joins the group when the young are old enough to venture out of the den. Observations on captive River Otters, however, show members of pairs to be very companionable the year around.

These animals have few natural enemies, except possibly when they are young. Their bodies are strong and muscular and they possess a keen sense of smell. Few other mammals would be likely to attack otters on land or be able to catch them in the water.

River Otters may be tamed and become quite friendly in captivity. Unlike various weasels and mink they make excellent pets.

SPOTTED SKUNK
Spilogale gracilis

Description — Total length, about 15 to 18 inches; tail length, 5 to 6½ inches. A small species of skunk with a white spot on the top of its head and 4 to 6 narrow longitudinal bands of white on the back and sides of the body. These bands tend to be broken up by the black background so as to produce a spotted effect. Underside of body, black. Tail, moderately bushy, especially tip which is white. Remainder of tail black except for a white spot at base. External ear, relatively small.

General Distribution—Occurs throughout much of the United States and in extreme southwestern British Columbia, south to Central America[1]. Rather widely distributed, at low or moderate elevations, throughout most of California and Nevada.

---

[1]The above given distributional range is that of the genus *Spilogale* which contains a number of currently recognized species. It appears likely that most, if not all, of these forms will upon further study prove to be subspecies of a single species. In such event the name *Spilogale putorius* will apply to the species, since this was the first described form of this now recognized genus.

Local Distribution — Not common in the Lake Tahoe region, but occurring in small numbers, locally, at lower elevations where dry and rocky, especially on the Nevada side.

Habits — Spotted Skunks are frequently referred to as "hydrophobia cats" and "civet cats," both incorrect names since members of this species are no more subject to rabies than many other mammals, and true civets are not native to the New World. Like their larger relatives, the Striped Skunks, these animals have well developed anal glands, capable of discharging their well-known musk for a distance of some feet. This, of course, is a protective mechanism resorted to only when in danger or suddenly frightened.

Except in very arid regions Spotted Skunks appear to be less numerous than Striped Skunks. This is particularly true about Lake Tahoe which is almost too high, altitudinally, for the smaller species.

Spotted Skunks show considerable preference for rocky canyons and outcrops, also for brushy slopes. These skunks are strictly nocturnal and inhabit hollow logs, rock piles, burrows or dens that are often made by other animals, and, not infrequently, houses and barns.

Their food consists largely of insects, especially beetles and grasshoppers, also mice and other small rodents, occasionally small birds and eggs. The long, pointed claws on the front feet are of considerable assistance in digging out insects and rodents.

Spotted Skunks have few enemies, although Horned Owls are reported to capture them occasionally. Their scent appears to be as obnoxious and irritating to other mammals as it is to man, consequently they are seldom molested by mammals that would normally prey on an animal of this size. The young are born in May or June and there are generally 4 to 6 in a litter.

The fur of the Spotted Skunk has a relatively low value so it is little sought after by trappers. Many are caught accidentally, however, in traps set for other animals.

Striped Skunk
Mephitis mephitis

Description — Total length, 24 to 28 inches; tail length, 10 to 13 inches. General size, about that of a house cat, with a stocky body, short legs, long front claws, a small head, small ears and a large bushy tail. Color, black with a narrow white mid-dorsal stripe extending from the base of the nose to the top of the head, and a broader white stripe extending from in back of the ears to the shoulder region where it divides into two stripes that continue to the base of the tail enclosing a black patch between them. A few of the hairs of the tail are entirely white but most of them have the basal half white and the distal half black. Fur, moderately long, with the coarser hairs possessing a decided luster.

General Distribution — From northern British Columbia, east to Nova Scotia, and south to northern Mexico. Widely distributed over California and Nevada, wherever water is available. Absent from areas of extreme aridity and from high mountainous country.

Local Distribution — Present in small numbers at lower elevations.

Habits — The Lake Tahoe basin is a little high, altitudinally, for Striped Skunks. They do occur there, however, in limited numbers and are occasionally trapped close to the shores of the lake.

Like the smaller Spotted Skunks, members of this species are most famous for their scent or musk, the odor of which is exceedingly strong and, if carried in the wind, may be detected for a distance of several miles. The faint odor of skunk is not unpleasant to many persons, but when concentrated is usually considered as obnoxious. The musk, or liquid secreted by the scent glands, is, of course, for self-protection and can be ejected by the animal with great rapidity and considerable accuracy for a distance of 8 to 10 feet. If it strikes the eyes it will produce temporary blindness and on contacting the skin may cause severe irritation.

Because of this effective means of self defense skunks are relatively indifferent to most other animals, including man. On a number of occasions when the writer has encountered these animals along trails they have rarely shown any signs of fear or for that matter paid much attention to the intruder who hastily granted them a right-of-way. When angry, skunks frequently stamp their front feet, and, if frightened, raise the tail in a threatening manner warning their attackers to beware.

Striped Skunks are principally nocturnal but not as strictly so as Spotted Skunks. Occasionally they are seen in the daytime and quite frequently are encountered in the early evening before dusk. They are not especially restricted to one type of habitat but are found in open forests, woodlands, brush, creek bottoms and meadowland. Suitable dens and food appear to be the principal determining factors governing their presence. Their dens are usually located in cavities or crevices in rocks, in hollow logs or beneath stumps. Frequently they appropriate the burrows of other animals, especially ground squirrels. The faint odor of skunk, plus the presence of a few of their long hairs, is usually a clue to the identity of the occupant of a suspected den. Unlike the Spotted Skunk, which is reported to climb trees at times, members of this species are strictly ground dwellers.

In many localities Striped Skunk appear to hole up and become inactive for a part of the winter, particularly during the periods of heavy rains or snow. This is true of members of this species in the Lake Tahoe region where their tracks are rarely noted from mid-December until spring when the snow begins to melt.

Insects and small rodents constitute the principal food of Striped Skunks. Occasionally they will eat reptiles, amphibians, birds, fruit, and berries. While skunks at times get into poultry yards and do considerable damage, they may generally be classified as very beneficial insect and rodent catchers, as well as valuable fur-bearers. Based upon the large number of pelts taken annually by trappers and the demand for Striped Skunk in the fur industry this species may be considered as one of our more valuable mammals.

The young are born in April or May and are naked and help-less at time of birth. The number in a litter varies from 2 to at least 9, although the average is about 5. They appear to be cared for entirely by the mother and even after they are old enough to forage for themselves follow her about for a long time.

Striped Skunks do not have many enemies but they are occasionally taken by foxes, Coyotes, Fishers and Horned Owls. There are even records of their capture by Golden Eagles. Unfortunately, because of their unsuspicious natures, they suffer greatly from poisoned baits placed out for other mammals. Sometimes this is indirectly acquired by eating rodents that have died from the effects of poisoned grain.

P & G MATTSON

AMERICAN BADGER
Taxidea taxus

Description — Total length, 2 to 2½ feet; tail, 5 to 6 inches long. Body, appearing broad and somewhat flattened. Back and sides, silvery-gray, sometimes with a brownish tinge. A narrow, white, mid-dorsal stripe of variable length present, extending from the base of the nose at least to the shoulder region and sometimes almost to the rump. Head, marked by alternating patches of black and white. Ears, proportionately small and rounded. Legs, short and black in coloration. Claws on front feet, very long (1 to 1½ inches) and only slightly curved. Tail, short but bushy.

General Distribution — From Alberta, Saskatchewan, and Manitoba south to central Mexico, east to Michigan and west to coastal California. Rather widely distributed over most of California and Nevada.

Local Distribution — Not common but found occasionally in open country, even alpine meadows.

Habits — The combination of a seemingly flattened body, long, silvery-gray fur, conspicuous white markings on the head, and long front claws make it unlikely that one would confuse a badger with any other animal.

This species has an exceptionally broad altitudinal range, extending from the lowest to nearly the highest parts of our country. Badgers usually avoid forested or rocky regions, showing a preference for open land inhabited by small rodents.

Their short but powerful legs and strong claws enable them to excavate for food with relative ease. Their presence, consequently, is more often known by the numerous large holes that they leave than by actual sight of the animals themselves. The rapidity with which badgers can dig is known to many persons. When cornered they have been observed to burrow out of sight in fairly hard ground in one minute and a half. A man or even a group of men equipped with shovels are generally unable to dig out a badger, so rapidly does it tunnel through the earth.

The front feet are used principally to loosen the soil in digging and frequently all four feet are employed in kicking the earth back. After penetrating a short distance beneath the surface badgers sometimes use the excavated soil to plug their burrows behind them as a protective measure. The entrances to their tunnels usually are broadly oval, conforming roughly to the low, broad shapes of their bodies. If the soil is sufficiently hard the deep telltale claw marks are invariably in evidence.

Badgers generally do not travel very far and seemingly do not require water. They are reported to remain in a favored locality until the small ground-dwelling rodent population is about cleaned out before moving to another suitable area. Pocket gophers and ground squirrels in many places constitute their principal food, although many other mammals and even reptiles and insects are eaten. When a badger captures an animal as large as a rabbit it generally digs a burrow at once and takes its food underground to eat. Although most active at night members of this species may be seen on occasions at any hour of the day.

Badgers are not known to hibernate, in the strict sense of the word, but they do den up for a time in winter in regions where there is an abundance of snow. The young are probably born in April and May in the higher mountains. The number in a litter varies from 1 to 4. They are reported to be weaned when about half-grown, although the mother brings them food until they are old enough to be on their own.

Because of their large size and strength badgers probably have few enemies apart from man. Like other members of the weasel family they possess anal scent glands capable of emitting a strong-smelling secretion if threatened with danger.

The value of badger fur was quite high in the 1920's, but has decreased considerably since then, although these animals are still classified as fur-bearers. Badgers are not very common at present. They are easily trapped and, unfortunately, fall easy victims to poisoned bait which is so often set out for Coyotes.

FAMILY CANIDAE — Foxes, Wolves, Coyotes

RED FOX
Vulpes fulva

Description — Total length, 3 to 3½ feet; tail length, about 14 inches. General coloration, varying from rich reddish-brown to blackish, depending upon whether in red, cross, silver or black color phase. Backs of ears and fronts of fore- and hind legs blackish, irrespective of body color. Tail, large, bushy, and always tipped with white.

General Distribution — From northern Alaska east to Newfoundland, south in eastern North America to southeastern United States; in western North America, south through the higher Rocky Mountains, the Cascades and the Sierra Nevada; locally, on certain high desert ranges in Nevada.

Local Distribution — Rare or at least of very limited occurrence in the higher mountains; occasionally reported near lake level.

Habits — The Red Fox of western United States, unlike its eastern relative, is usually an inhabitant of remote, high mountain regions where it attempts to avoid man and his habitations. It is familiar only to a few hardy trappers who occasionally brave the rigors of an alpine winter.

A simple description of the color of this species is not easy because of its several pelage phases. These phases are neither seasonal nor, in the true sense, geographic in occurrence but rather are comparable to the color phases of the Black Bear. That is to say, they may all occur within one litter in a family, although the relative abundance of any one phase may vary with locality. Silvers and blacks are much more common in the far North than they are in the Sierra Nevada where the cross and red phases predominate. None of these color varieties, however, are sharply defined or set off from one another but rather show a gradual blending. Thus one may find almost any intermediate variation from the typical red to the so-called black, many of which are difficult to allocate to one particular color phase.

Red Foxes have been reported as observed or captured at a number of localities in the Lake Tahoe region including the following: along the Velma Lakes Trail south of Eagle Lake, the head of Ward Creek near Twin Peaks, Marlette Lake, Sandy Point, and two miles south of Glenbrook.

In the high Sierra Nevada these animals are believed to live in rocky dens instead of occupying burrows in the ground as do their eastern relatives. During the summer Red Foxes often range well above timber line. Some trappers are of the opinion that, at least in certain localities, there is a slight downward migration in winter, perhaps induced by the seasonal scarcity of available food at very high elevations.

Red Foxes live on a number of different kinds of small animals. In some places White-tailed Jack Rabbits constitute a major part of their food but, in general, chipmunks, squirrels, wood rats, and mice are equally important and occasionally birds are captured.

In winter, when travel over the snow is difficult, the pads of the feet of members of this species are covered by the dense fur that grows between them. This serves to increase the surface of the feet, somewhat like a snowshoe. The tracks of these animals, therefore, are ill-defined at this season. These hairs gradually wear off and by summer the naked pads of the sole and toes are exposed.

The breeding season for Red Foxes in the Sierra Nevada is said to begin about the middle of February and the gestation period for the species is 51 days. A litter of young may vary from 3 to 9 individuals. The males of this species, unlike those of many other carnivores, are said to assist in caring for the young.

The Red Fox has a voice that is somewhat louder than that of the Gray Fox of the low country. Like the latter, however, it barks instead of howling like the Coyote.

These animals have relatively few natural enemies but are captured occasionally by Bobcats and Golden Eagles.

While selected Red Fox pelts, particularly in the black and silver phases, still command a good price and have sold in the past for as much as one thousand dollars, the production of these animals in fur farms has tended to decrease their commercial value greatly in recent years.

Coyote
Canis latrans

Description—Total length, 4 to 4½ feet; tail length, 12 inches or slightly more. In general appearance, resembling a slender shepherd dog. Color above, grizzled buffy-gray and black. Underparts, whitish. Ears, pointed. Tail, large, bushy, and usually black at the tip.

General Distribution—From the Mt. McKinley District of Alaska south to southern Mexico; east to the northern Mississippi Valley and Texas.

Local Distribution—Fairly common from lake level to above timber line.

Habits—There is hardly any place about the shores of Lake Tahoe or in the surrounding country where one in the course of a few nights will fail to hear the high-pitched howls of the Coyote. Sometimes a single animal will call, at other times there will be a chorus, seemingly joined in by individuals from every direction. It is a weird wild sound sufficient to chill the blood of the inexperienced camper, but is always a thrill to those who love the wilderness and its inhabitants.

One cannot very well define or limit the habitat occupied by members of this species since they range from the deserts to the mountain tops in western North America. In the Lake Tahoe region I have seen coyote tracks as abundant in the mud of Rowlands Marsh as on the crests of the highest peaks surrounding the lake basin. Perhaps broken country with forest, brush and meadowland intermingled might be considered as presenting the optimum conditions for the species in this area.

Coyotes are active principally at night but it is not unusual to see them in the daytime. One day early in July, 1937, while we were watching Pikas just west of the summit of Genoa Peak, a large Coyote came into sight and passed within 20 yards of one of our party who was about 150 yards from me. This person whistled to attract my attention but the animal which was to the windward seemed unaware of any human presence. It trotted behind a small ridge and soon came into sight again about 40 yards from me. Finally it stopped, poised with its front feet on a rock, and looked down the slope toward us. It soon became aware of our presence and, after a moment's hesitation, lowered its body and seemed to sneak over the top of the ridge. A later investigation of its tracks on the northeastern slope of the ridge, which was still covered with deep snow, revealed that when once out of our sight it had run very rapidly. Great bounds had carried it as much as 10 feet at a time down the slope.

Coyotes frequently dig their own burrows where the ground is soft or sandy, but in rocky country crevices or dens in the rocks serve equally well. The young, 3 to 11 in number, are born in these burrows or dens and, according to the reports of reliable observers, are tended only by the mother. The male parent, however, may bring food to the vicinity of his mate and young, although he does not directly present it to the latter. The breeding season may start as early as January. The young are usually born in April and May and by June they are old enough to hunt for themselves.

Coyotes sometimes hunt in small packs or groups but for the most part they are seen alone. Their principal natural food consists of small rodents, particularly mice, pocket gophers and squirrels. These are generally dug out of the ground or secured by stalking. Rabbits are also important items in the diet of Coyotes and on occasions, if food is scarce, larger animals such as deer may be captured. Coyotes are not restricted entirely to a meat diet. When the snow is deep in the high mountains in winter and rodents are difficult to find they have even been known to consume juniper berries for subsistence.

Although Coyotes may hole up for a few days during a heavy snow storm they do not hibernate. In certain localities there appears to be a downward movement of mountain populations in winter, probably due to the scarcity of food at higher levels.

Coyotes, because of their size, strength and wariness, have few enemies, aside from man. The slow-moving but formidable porcupine, however, has accounted for the deaths of many of these larger animals. The remains of Coyotes with numerous porcupine quills embedded in the mouth and other parts of the head have attested to the ultimate death of the victor as well as the vanquished.

This species may be classed as an important fur-bearer in the West and the trapping and sale of Coyote pelts is a major means of obtaining a livelihood for a number of persons. The local control of Coyotes in sheep-raising areas is frequently necessary but it is unfortunate that such measures are often carried on in remote areas where these animals are both beneficial as a means of naturally curbing rodent populations as well as valuable for their pelts when properly taken in winter.

FAMILY FELIDAE—Cats

P&G MATTSON

MOUNTAIN LION
Felis concolor

Description—Total length, 6 to 8 feet; tail length, 2 to nearly 3 feet. General appearance, cat-like, with head small in proportion to body size. Color, varying from tawny-brown to grayish-brown above, paler beneath. Backs of ears and tip of tail, blackish-brown. Ears, lacking tufts. Tail, cylindrical. Claws, retractile.

General Distribution—From northern British Columbia in North America south to Patagonia in South America. Eliminated or greatly reduced throughout much of its former range.

Local Distribution—Sufficiently rare as to be classed as a straggler in the region.

Habits—The Mountain Lion is the second largest cat in the Western Hemisphere, exceeded in size only by the Jaguar which ranges from e xt r e m e southwestern United States into South America. Numerous names have been applied to this species such as Cougar, Panther, Painter, Puma and Catamount but it is probably best known as the Mountain Lion.

Despite their large size and great strength these animals are rarely seen, even in regions where they are relatively numerous and even there one has little to fear from them. To be sure there have been several authenticated cases in the history of North America in which Mountain Lions have been known to kill humans. Such instances, however, are extremely rare. The victims have usually been children and the offenders old or crippled animals that were seriously handicapped in obtaining their usual food.

Mountain Lions are of rare occurrence in the Lake Tahoe region or anywhere along the eastern side of the Sierra Nevada. Stragglers, probably from the lower western slopes have, however, occasionally drifted in. One is recorded as having been seen and later shot at Spooner in the winter of 1934 (Hall, 1946, p. 273). In August, 1935, I was informed by the superintendent of a C. C. C. Camp that tracks of a lion had recently been found within the boundary of D. L. Bliss State Park at Rubicon Point and that similar tracks had been noted the previous autumn.

In general, Mountain Lions are inhabitants of forested or chaparral-covered country at middle altitudes. Each animal ranges over many miles and may follow rather definite circuits, though it may be several weeks before it returns over the same route. They are usually solitary and have their dens in natural cavities between boulders, in rock slides, at the base of hollow trees or in other similarly protected places.

Many disputes have arisen over the voice of the Mountain Lion and tales are still prevalent regarding its ability to scream like a human in distress. Few of these stories have ever been substantiated and in most instances it appears that the sounds, supposedly attributed to lions, were produced by other animals. The general concensus of opinion is that Mountain Lions are singularly silent animals and call but rarely. They are, however, definitely known to growl, hiss, spit, mew and purr, especially when young.

Among Mountain Lions, as is true of many other carnivores, the males are decidedly larger than the females. The average female weighs less than 100 pounds and the average male less than 165 pounds, although there are seemingly authenticated records of exceptionally large males that have weighed in excess of 200 pounds.

Deer constitute the principal food of Mountain Lions in western United States. The great stealth, power and protective coloring of these big cats admirably adapt them to prey upon such large forest- or chaparral-inhabiting herbivores. Unable to run fast for more than a short distance, lions usually capture their game by lying in wait at suitable points along trails or by stalking. Such kills are often carried a considerable distance before being eaten. The remains are sometimes covered with sticks or twigs and returned to again. Although mountain lions depend principally on deer for food, many other animals are also eaten, including various kinds of rabbits, Porcupines, Bobcats, wood rats, mice and at times, even domestic stock.

Since there is no definite mating season the young may be born during any month of the year. The number in a litter varies from 1 to 4. Young lions at time of birth weigh approximately one pound and are about 12 inches in total length. Their fur is marked with small, irregular, dark spots and their tails are banded or barred. These markings disappear when they are from 4 to 12 months of age. The young are weaned when from 4 to 5 weeks old and are soon trained by their mother in hunting methods. Sometimes their training starts on grasshoppers, although it ultimately ends with deer. The young remain with their mother for a long time, occasionally more than a year. The male parent has nothing to do with the care of his offspring.

The Mountain Lion has essentially no natural enemies in this country. Man, however, in his desire to carry on predatory animal control, has exterminated or greatly reduced the lion population throughout much of its former range.

P&G MATTSON

BOBCAT
Lynx rufus

Description—Total length, 2½ to 3 feet; tail length, about 6 inches. Upper parts, grayish or reddish-brown. Fore- and hind legs, with distinct blackish spots. Underparts, white with black spots. Fur, soft and moderately long, especially on belly. Ears, possessing conspicuous black tufts of fur on their tips. Tail, short, white beneath to tip, and with black bars present on upper distal portion. Hind legs, long in porportion to size of body. Claws, retractile.

General Distribution—From southern Canada south throughout United States to south-central Mexico.

Local Distribution—Not common but occasionally found in rocky canyons or brushy slopes, particularly in the eastern part of the Tahoe region.

Habits—The Bobcat, Wildcat or Lynx Cat is a smaller relative of the northern Canada Lynx. It is a species with a very wide range as regards altitude and habitat, especially in western United States where it is found from the sea coast to the higher mountains and from the humid northwestern forests to the southern deserts. Bobcats do, however, show some preference for rocky canyons and dense brush.

While they are nocturnal in general it is not unusual to see individuals out hunting by daylight, particularly in the late afternoon. Bobcats follow rather definite circuits and frequently cover a distance of 4 or 5 miles during a single night. Their dens or lairs are most often located among rocks or in dense brush.

The voice of these cats is said to resemble that of a house cat but is somewhat deeper. Yowling is most often heard during the mating season. In addition to this they can hiss, spit and growl like most members of the cat tribe.

Since most of their hunting is done on the ground Bobcats live principally on ground-dwelling species. Rabbits, ground squirrels, pocket gophers, wood rats, mice, as well as quail and other small birds all serve as food. There are also occasional reports of their capturing deer, particularly in winter.

The young are born between February and September, although most of the kittens appear in April or May. While 3 is the usual number in a litter it may vary from 1 to 4. The young of this species, like the kittens of domestic cats, do not have their eyes open at time of birth and are dependent upon their mother until they are several months old.

Bobcats have few or no important natural enemies among the mammals. There are authenticated records of their capture by Mountain Lions but such occurrences must be very rare. Although the average Bobcat weighs less than 20 pounds it is a powerful animal and a formidable foe not likely to be attacked even by members of larger predatory species.

ORDER RODENTIA—Rodents or Gnawing Mammals

FAMILY SCIURIDAE—Marmots, Squirrels, etc.

P&GM

YELLOW-BELLIED MARMOT
Marmot flaviventris

Description—Total length, 22 to 28 inches; tail length, 5 to 8 inches. Body, proportionately heavy with legs relatively short. General color of back and sides, grizzled brown, becoming paler on rump. Top and sides of head, blackish, with patches of white in front of the eyes, on either side of nose, and on chin. Sides of neck, legs and underparts, yellowish-brown. Tail, short, moderately bushy, brown in color.

General Distribution—From south-central British Columbia south through the Rocky Mountains to New Mexico; south also through the Cascades and mountains of eastern Washington and Oregon to the southern Sierra Nevada in California and the higher ranges of central Nevada.

Local Distribution—Occurs principally at higher elevations in the Tahoe region, especially about rock slides or boulders along the margins of alpine meadows.

Habits—Three species of marmots occur in North America and are variously referred to in different regions by the names woodchuck, groundhog, whistler or siffleur. The term marmot, however, is most commonly used for the species occurring in California and Nevada. It is the largest member of the squirrel family in the Sierra Nevada and, because of its size, is frequently mistaken for some carnivore when first seen. In certain respects it bears a slight resemblance to a badger although members of the two species differ decidedly in color, behavior and, as a general rule, with respect to the type of habitat occupied.

Marmots are not often seen in the lower parts of the Tahoe basin, although they do occur along the rocky slopes of the gorge through which the Truckee River flows and about the head of Emerald Bay, near Eagle Falls. They are not uncommon, however, above 8000 feet and may even be found above timber line on the higher peaks. Here they most often frequent rock slides occupied by other mammals, such as Pikas, Bushy-tailed Wood Rats, Pine Martens and weasels. Sometimes they will be found along the margins of alpine meadows where they live in burrows, usually beneath large boulders. These burrows are dug by the occupants themselves and have a diameter of about 6 inches.

Marmots, like most members of the family to which they belong, are active only during the daytime. They may frequently be seen stretched out on the tops of flat boulders basking in the sun. Even when the animals themselves are not in evidence their droppings are usually to be found in such places. The call note of this species is a loud whistle which carries for a considerable distance.

The food of marmots consists principally of grass, green herbs and shrubs. In the late summer and early autumn their bodies accumulate a great deal of fat in preparation for the long winter sleep that is soon to follow. By late August or September they go into hibernation and in the high mountains rarely emerge before the end of April. In 1927 the "first marmot of the season" was seen on April 28 along the Truckee River.

Little is known of the breeding habits of the Yellow-bellied Marmot in this region apart from the fact that the young are born in the early summer. The number in a litter may vary from 3 to 8.

Although groundhogs in the East may cause considerable loss to the farmer and accordingly are sometimes considered as pests, the marmots of the Sierra Nevada hardly ever come into conflict with man since they occur at such high elevations in the mountains. Their large size and loud whistle make them objects of attraction to those who are fortunate enough to have the opportunity of observing them while visiting the high country.

BELDING GROUND SQUIRREL
Citellus beldingi

Description—Total length, 10 to 12 inches; tail length, 2½ to 3 inches. Body, more or less rat-like in appearance with ears proportionately small and tail relatively short and scantily haired.

General color, grayish-yellow with a broad brownish band extending from the nape region to the rump. Underparts, more creamy-gray in appearance. Tail, grayish-brown above, bright reddish-brown beneath.

General Distribution—From eastern Oregon and southwestern Idaho south through parts of northern and central Nevada, northeastern California and the Sierra Nevada south to the headwaters of the Kings River in Fresno County.

Local Distribution—Fairly common in grassy meadows throughout the Tahoe region, except where eliminated by man.

Habits—Belding Ground Squirrels are common inhabitants of meadowland in the Lake Tahoe region. On rare occasions they may be found about rocks or in very open forests but such situations are not usual for members of this species. In former years these animals were abundant in most of the grassy meadows close to the lake shore and along the Truckee River but "poison campaigns" carried on against our native mammals recently by various agencies have produced a marked decrease and even complete elimination of the squirrel populations in many places. In the higher mountain meadows as well as in parts of Lake Valley these animals are still fairly common.

The alarm notes of Belding Ground Squirrels are very characteristic and, when once known, serve as a ready means of quickly determining their presence in a region. The calls consist of a series of about 6 or 8 short, shrill, rapidly repeated notes which may be uttered either when running or when standing erect. The latter posture, with the body in a vertical position, resting on the soles of the hind feet, is responsible for the term "picket-pin" which is so often applied to these squirrels.

Belding Ground Squirrels live in burrows which they dig for themselves. Each appears to have its own burrow system although these are often located close together. They do not climb trees such as many other species of ground squirrels do on occasion and are rarely even seen on rocks. Their food consists almost entirely of grass.

Generally, about the end of September these animals go into hibernation and do not emerge until the following spring. In 1927 the first Belding Ground Squirrel was noted on April 26 in a meadow near the mouth of Burton Creek.

The young are born in June and July and usually number 5 or 6 to a litter. Within several weeks after birth the young may be seen outside the burrows and by late summer immature ground squirrels appear to outnumber the adults, judging by those seen above ground. Before they are full grown they have excavated their own burrows and are shifting for themselves. As far as known the females bear only one litter a year.

The principal natural enemies that Belding Ground Squirrels have to fear are weasels, badgers and Coyotes all of which prey upon these little ground dwellers.

CALIFORNIA GROUND SQUIRREL

Citellus beecheyi

Description—Total length 16 to 19 inches; tail length, 5 to 7½ inches. A fairly large-sized ground squirrel with moderately small ears and a proportionately long, well-haired tail. General color, grayish-brown with dappling present over much of the back and sides. A grizzled gray triangular patch present on each side of the body in the neck and shoulder region. Eye, surrounded by a whitish ring. Underparts of body, grayish-yellow without any dappling.

General Distribution—The Pacific coast region of North America from the Columbia River in Oregon south to northern Lower California, extending eastward as far as west-central Nevada.

Local Distribution—Widely distributed, though not sufficiently numerous as to be classed abundant, at lower elevations in the lake basin.

Habits—Most persons are likely to associate the California Ground Squirrel with the valley and foothill regions west of the main body of the Sierra Nevada because it is principally here that this species has shown such a marked population increase since the settlement of the West by man. It is unfortunate indeed for the agriculturist that so many of his efforts at land utilization have proved favorable to this native rodent. The reduction in the numbers of some of the natural enemies of these animals, such as Golden Eagles and several kinds of broad-winged hawks as well as certain carnivorous mammals, may also be a factor responsible in part for their increase. Today the artificial control of ground squirrels is a necessity in many farming areas because of the upset in nature's balance that inevitably accompanies advancing civilization.

While the California Ground Squirrel is most numerous and conspicuous in the valley and foothill country, it ranges well up into the Sierra Nevada on both the eastern and western slopes. About Lake Tahoe one may frequently observe these squirrels, although they are confined largely to lower elevations about the vicinity of the lake shore and even there are outnumbered by the Golden-mantled Ground Squirrel. No problem of overpopulation has arisen in this region nor is it likely to do so in the future since it is largely above the altitudinal level of tolerance for the species.

Since open, well-drained grasslands or plains, so favored by members of this species in the low country, are largely lacking in the Lake Tahoe region, the California Ground Squirrels in this mountainous area must select other available situations for home sites. They are most often seen in open forests or loose brush near boulders or talus slides and their burrows are constructed beneath the protective covering of such rocks.

The seasonal activity of this species of ground squirrel appears to vary considerably with locality. Where a temperate climate prevails, as in parts of coastal California, some ground squirrels may remain active the year around. Frequently, however, the adults become inactive in late summer and during the coldest part of the winter. In regions where the summer temperatures are higher and the winter temperatures lower the period of dormancy may continue through from late summer to late winter. In the higher Sierra Nevada where there is snow for a number of months in the year dormancy may extend from October or November to March or April.

Ground squirrels are capable of feeding on a wide variety of native and non-native plants. Given the opportunity, they will occasionally take meat and eggs. Grasses and herbaceous plants constitute the principal food eaten in the spring and early summer. Later in the year seeds, nuts and berries are of major importance in this regard.

Little is known concerning the reproduction of ground squirrels in the Tahoe region but in view of the extended period of dormancy in the spring it appears that the young are not born until May or June. It is generally believed that the period of gestation is between 25 and 30 days. The young are born in a nest chamber lined with dry grass in the mother's burrow. They are about six weeks old before they make their first excursion into the outer world. The number of young in a litter varies considerably. Extremes of 4 and 17 have been recorded, but the average is probably about 7. By the end of summer young squirrels generally leave the mother's burrow and each establishes its own home.

Because it has been responsible for many serious economic losses in agricultural areas this species of rodent has been the subject of several intensive life history studies. The reader is referred to the detailed accounts of Linsdale (1946), Storer (1942) and Grinnell and Dixon (1918) for further information.

P&G MATTSON

GOLDEN-MANTLED GROUND SQUIRREL
Citellus lateralis

Description—Total length 9½ to 11 inches; tail length, 3 to 4 inches. Body, porportionally short and stocky, with ears moderately small. Three longitudinal stripes present on either side of back, one whitish, bordered on either side by a black stripe. A broad, grizzled band of grayish-brown extending down center of back from behind shoulders to base of tail. Sides and underparts of body, behind the shoulders and chest, yellowish-gray. Top and sides of head, neck and shoulders, bright cinnamon or russet-brown in fresh pelage, becoming more yellowish in worn pelage. Chin and underside of neck and chest, somewhat paler. Tail, brownish-black above and rich reddish-brown below.

General Distribution—Most of the higher mountains of western North America from eastern British Columbia and western Alberta south to New Mexico and Arizona. Occurs in California on the high, inner, north coast ranges, the Sierra Nevada, the White Mountains and the San Bernardino Mountains. Found on most of the higher ranges in Nevada.

Local Distribution—Common and of widespread occurrence from lake level to timber line, showing preference, however, for open forests, particularly where rocks and fallen timber are present.

Habits—This is probably the most abundant and widely distributed species of ground squirrel in the high Sierra Nevada. With the exception of the chipmunks, Golden-mantled Ground Squirrels, or Copperheads as they are sometimes called, are better known to most Lake Tahoe visitors than any of the other native mammals. They may be found nearly anywhere from the well-inhabited shores of the lake to the upper limits of tree growth, shunning only extensive, open meadowland.

Since Golden-mantled Ground Squirrels prefer forest cover they are fairly common about most of the public camps located in such situations. A few scraps of bread regularly placed out will almost invariably be a means of rapidly cultivating a friendship with them.

These squirrels are not infrequently confused with chipmunks because of their stripes. Their pictures are present on numerous post cards with the title "Lake Tahoe Chipmunk" below. However, their larger size, coppery head lacking stripes, and the absence of a dark stripe down the center of the back readily distinguish them from their smaller, more nimble relatives.

Golden-mantled Ground Squirrels frequently climb over large rocks but only on rare occasions may be seen in trees. They are true ground dwellers and dig their burrows in the soil, usually under the edges of boulders or fallen logs.

Along the margins of meadows one may frequently see Belding and Golden-mantled Ground Squirrels together, but the latter species rarely ventures far into the open where its larger relative is most at home. Likewise, at lower elevations near the lake these squirrels are sometimes seen with California Ground Squirrels.

Unlike most diurnal members of the squirrel family this species is notably silent. Occasionally, however, one may be heard giving a high-pitched call note.

The food of Golden-mantled Ground Squirrels consists principally of seeds secured from a wide variety of plants, ranging from small annuals to coniferous trees. By autumn their bodies have acquired a considerable amount of fat so as to tide them through the period of hibernation which begins about the first of October. The latest seasonal date on which this species has been observed above ground in this region is October 6 (Howell, 1938, p. 32). By the middle of the following April a few individuals may be observed above ground and by the end of that month they are once again commonly in evidence.

Not much is known about the breeding habits of Golden-mantled Ground Squirrels other than that the young are born in early summer and usually number 4 to 6 in a litter. By the middle of summer many of the half-grown young may be seen above the ground.

Members of this species are of little economic importance since, for the most part, they inhabit regions that are unsuitable for agricultural purposes.

Like other small ground-dwelling rodents of the high mountains these squirrels are preyed upon by weasels, Coyotes, Pine Martens and other carnivorous mammals. Among the predatory birds the Cooper Hawk and Goshawk are their most serious enemies since both are forest-inhabiting species.

CHIPMUNKS

YELLOW PINE CHIPMUNK

Eutamias amoenas

Description—Total length, 7½ to 8½ inches; tail length, 3 to 3¾ inches. General color pattern, similar to that of the three other species of chipmunks recorded from the Lake Tahoe region, with five longitudinal brownish-black stripes alternating with four whitish stripes on the back, a light grayish or whitish patch behind each ear, and three blackish and two whitish stripes on either side of the head. The top of the head and the rump region are a grizzled gray-brown and the sides of the body are bright reddish-brown. The tail is proportionately long, appears rather flattened although bushy, and is of approximately a uniform width.

This species can be distinguished from the Townsend and Long-eared chipmunks by its considerably smaller size and by the yellowish rather than reddish color on the underside of the tail. The Yellow Pine Chipmunk closely resembles the Lodgepole Chipmunk from which it differs in being slightly smaller, showing less contrast between the light and dark stripes, having the central pair of white stripes on the back generally broader than the outer pair and in having a more pronounced yellowish wash on the light facial stripes as well as on the hairs on the ventral parts of the body. These two species, however, are difficult to distinguish from each other in the field.

General Distribution—Western North America from central British Columbia south to Wyoming, southern Idaho, northern and extreme western Nevada and the central Sierra Nevada in California.

Local Distribution—Common throughout most of the Lake Tahoe region, occurring both in forest and brushland; while most abundant near lake level individuals may occasionally be found almost up to timber line.

LODGEPOLE CHIPMUNK
Eutamias speciosus

Description—Total length, 7¾ to 8¾ inches; tail length, 3 to 4 inches. This species is very similar in general appearance to the Yellow Pine Chipmunk from which it may be distinguished by its slightly larger size, more contrasting light and dark stripes, by the proportionately narrower central pair of white stripes on the back, and by the reduction or absence of a yellowish wash to the light facial stripes and hairs on the underparts of the body.

General Distribution—The Sierra Nevada of California and extreme western Nevada, south in California on certain higher mountain ranges to the San Jacinto Mountains in Riverside County.

Local Distribution—Occurs widely throughout the Tahoe region but usually found in or close to coniferous forests, especially lodgepole pine.

TOWNSEND CHIPMUNK
Eutamias townsendi

Description—Total length, 9 to 10½ inches; tail length, 3½ to 4¾ inches. This species is readily distinguished from the Yellow Pine and Lodgepole chipmunks by its larger size, by the presence of brownish rather than blackish stripes on the back and by a reddish-brown rather than yellowish-brown color on the underside of the tail. From the nearly related Long-eared Chipmunk this species may be distinguished by its slightly larger size, smaller ears, and generally duller coloration.

General Distribution—From s o u t h e r n British Columbia south through western Washington and Oregon to central California along the coast and in the Sierra Nevada; in Nevada only in the region of Lake Tahoe.

Local Distribution—Said to show preference for mature stands of conifers or logged or burned areas where large logs and stumps remain.

LONG-EARED CHIPMUNK
Eutamias quadrimaculatus

Description—Total length, 8½ to 9¾ inches; tail length, 3¼ to 4½ inches. This species is easily separated from the Yellow Pine and Lodgepole chipmunks on the basis of its larger size, by the presence of more conspicuous white patches behind the ears and by the color of the tail which is a rich reddish-brown beneath and has white-tipped rather than buffy-tipped hairs along the lateral margins. From the Townsend Chipmunk this species is most readily distinguished by its larger ears with more prominent white patches behind them, and more nearly white lateral body and cheek stripes.

General Distribution—Limited to the northern and central Sierra Nevada in California and extreme western Nevada.

Local Distribution—Occurs in brush and open forest usually below the 8000-foot level.

HABITS

It would be a difficult feat indeed to travel very far through the mountainous portions of western United States without soon becoming acquainted with one or more kinds of chipmunks. They are almost as much a part of the scene as the coniferous forests in which they dwell. Not all chipmunks, of course, are restricted to the mountains or for that matter to tree growth of any sort. However, it is with the pines and firs that we commonly associate these diminutive striped members of the squirrel family.

Four kinds of chipmunks occur in the Lake Tahoe region. They are so similar, however, in general appearance and in habits that it is difficult for the amateur to tell them apart. The larger, heavier bodied Townsend and Long-eared chipmunks are less numerous and generally of more local occurrence than are members of the two smaller species. In the author's experience the Lodgepole Chipmunk is more widely distributed throughout this area than any of the others, occurring from lake level to timber line. Likewise, it is more often found in trees, sometimes even living in deserted woodpecker holes a good many feet above the ground in old snags.

Chipmunks are most nearly related to ground squirrels and, like the latter, possess storage pouches in their cheeks. They are strictly diurnal, becoming active about sunrise and retiring to their nests in the late afternoon when a chill in the air foretells the approach of evening. During the day they may be seen or heard as they scamper across the forest floor, over logs and stumps, or through clumps of small trees and brush. Much of their time is devoted to collecting and storing food. The call notes of chipmunks are soon recognized by the camper as these little creatures dash about his temporary premises in search of crumbs and other edibles that may have dropped accidentally to the ground or been placed there on purpose to cultivate a friendship. Sometimes the call is a loud "whisk," given with a simultaneous flip of the tail. It may be a low "chuck" which is often repeated, after nearly equal intervals of several seconds, until it becomes monotonous. When a chipmunk is suddenly surprised it may utter a series of chuckling notes as it dashes to cover.

Nuts, berries and seeds constitute the principal food of chipmunks. Early in the season the seeds of many annual plants and grasses are sought after. Later, in the summer, when the manzanita and ceanothus fruits are mature, chipmunks seem to spend their entire days climbing through these bushes as they harvest the crop. The seeds of most of the conifers are highly prized by these animals. They frequently eat various kinds of fungi, like many other members of the squirrel family.

Much of the food that is gathered during the day is stored in caches for future use. Small excavations are made in the ground after which the accumulated seeds in the cheek-pouches of the digger are removed and placed in the hole, then rapidly covered. Each individual constructs so many of these small caches, when food is plentiful, that it seems impossible that they could all be found again. No doubt many are overlooked and the buried seeds ultimately germinate, thus insuring the future of the forest. Larger items of food, such as fungi, even pieces of bread secured from visitors, are often stored in the crotches of small trees, a habit somewhat resembling that of the Red Squirrel.

Chipmunks live principally in holes which they construct themselves in the forest floor or in brushland. The entrances to these burrows are usually rather inconspicuous, not being marked by a large pile of earth like those of many ground squirrels. Some believe that the end through which the earth has been excavated is closed permanently upon completion of the burrow and a new entrance or entrances are made. Holes in old stumps and fallen snags, even old woodpecker holes in standing snags frequently serve as home sites for these animals.

As far as known all of the chipmunks in the Tahoe region go into dormancy during the winter. They are rarely seen from November to late March and are not out in abundance in the spring until well on in April.

The breeding season starts in May and most of the young are born in June. A litter generally consists of from 3 to 6 individuals. The young grow rapidly and may be seen out in numbers foraging for themselves by July or early August.

Chipmunks, like most small terrestrial rodents, have many enemies. Cooper Hawks, Sharp-shinned Hawks, even Goshawks and Red-tailed Hawks may prey upon them, if given the opportunity. Most of the smaller carnivorous mammals may occasionally catch chipmunks but of all these the weasels are probably their most serious enemies. More than once has the author observed weasels carrying chipmunks in their mouths. Rattlesnakes also frequently feed upon these animals.

P & G MATTSON

RED SQUIRREL
Tamiasciurus douglasii

Description—Total length, 12 to 14 inches; tail length, 4½ to 5½ inches. Upper parts, dark grayish-brown. Underparts, white or sometimes, slightly tinged with buff. Each side of the body marked by a narrow longitudinal band of black separating the dark upper parts from the light underparts. Ears, slightly tufted with brownish-black hairs. Tops of front and hind feet, orange-brown. Tail, bushy, appearing somewhat flattened, blackish-brown in color, with the tips of the hairs along the margins white.

General Distribution—From southern British Columbia south through western Washington and Oregon to the southern Sierra Nevada in California and in the mountains of northern Lower California, Mexico.

Local Distribution—Found throughout the forested parts of the Lake Tahoe region.

Habits—Like chipmunks, the Red Squirrels, or Chickarees as they are often called, are a conspicuous part of the forest life about Lake Tahoe. Although occasionally seen foraging on the ground these squirrels are truly arboreal. They can run straight up the trunks of trees, seemingly with effortless grace, or skillfully travel through the branches, jumping from tree to tree.

Red Squirrels are active the year around but only during the daylight hours. Frequently, during the middle of the day or in the early afternoon, one will be seen stretched out asleep on a large limb or even on a fallen log. At night they retire to holes in trees. Their calls may be heard nearly any time during the day from near or far in the forest. The commonest call is a series of rapidly repeated notes having the mechanical quality of a muffled alarm clock ringing. Sometimes, especially when curious but wary, they emit an explosive bark and, occasionally when chasing each other, they make a number of chuckling notes.

The seeds of coniferous trees form the principal food of Red Squirrels in this region. Much of their time during the summer and autumn months is devoted to harvesting pine and fir cones. When engaged in this sort of activity a squirrel will usually cut a number of cones, either green or ripe, from the crown of a tree and allow them to drop to the ground. Let the camper beware if he is so unfortunate as to be located beneath a heavily cone-laden tree at this season because falling cones can be a serious menace.

After a number of these have been dropped the squirrel will descend to the ground for further action. Some may be carried to storage sites, others may be taken to a log or up to a limb where they will rapidly be taken apart and the nuts eaten.

Large numbers of these cones are stored at various places in the forest, usually at the bases of trees or next to fallen logs, for winter use. The "kitchen middens" or piles of cone scales one frequently sees in the woods indicate places where Red Squirrels regularly dismantle cones when feeding. In winter when the ground is covered with snow they frequently excavate to reach their caches. Various forest fungi also provide Red Squirrels with food. These too are sometimes stored, but usually in the crotches of trees where they will dry.

The young of this species are generally born in June and July. Ordinarily by the end of August they may be seen running about in numbers. Five is probably the average number in a litter. The nest in which the young are born and reared is usually an old woodpecker hole that has been renovated and lined with shredded bark, cone scales and other plant material.

Red Squirrels are of no direct commercial value in western North America. Their fur is not sought after by trappers nor can these animals legally be taken for such purposes in California. Their flesh is tough and strong, quite unlike that of their relatives the Gray Squirrels. However, they are important as a source of food for several kinds of fur-bearing mammals. They also play a rôle in forest reproduction by planting the seeds of many coniferous trees. Last, but not least, by their very presence they add to the attractiveness of the mountain forests for members of the human species.

Cooper Hawks, G o s h a w k s, even Red-tailed Hawks and Horned Owls have been known to prey upon these squirrels. Among mammals the Pine Marten is probably their most serious enemy, especially in the higher country where marten are fairly numerous.

Northern Flying Squirrel
Glaucomys sabrinus

Description—Total length, 11 to 12 inches; tail length, 4½ to 5½ inches. Fur on upper parts of body and head, soft buffy-gray in color and very silky in texture. Head, quite round, with eyes proportionately large. Front and hind legs connected by a fur-covered membrane which extends out laterally from the side of the body. Tail, bushy, but very flattened in appearance, with the hairs on the upper side dark gray and lacking in luster. Underparts of body and tail, whitish tinged with buff.

General Distribution—From central and southeastern Alaska east to Nova Scotia and south to northern United States, except in the West where the range of the species extends southwards, in suitable localities, to the San Bernardino and San Jacinto mountains of southern California.

Local Distribution—Not uncommon in forested areas, especially where there are red firs.

Habits—The average visitors or even residents of the Lake Tahoe region are probably less familiar with this species than any other members of the squirrel family occurring here. Actually there is little doubt but that the flying squirrel population in this area exceeds the combined populations of the Yellow-bellied Marmot and Belding Ground Squirrel and trapping records indicate that in certain favorable localities it is almost equal to that of the Red Squirrel. Members of this species, however, are arboreal, nocturnal, shy and relatively silent, hence they are only rarely seen by man.

Flying squirrels are not capable of true flight but are gliders. Their light, flattened bodies with broad membranes extending out laterally and connecting with their fore- and hind feet present a broad surface for sailing through the air for a considerable distance. Their fur is very soft and silky in texture. Perhaps this is a means of reducing friction or resistance to air while gliding. Tree squirrels, in general, have large bushy tails which serve as balancing organs when these animals are running along slender branches or leaping from limb to limb. The tail of the flying squirrel, in addition to being bushy, is flattened so that the hairs appear to come out laterally. This flattened type of tail serves not only to increase the gliding surface but performs a function similar to that accomplished by the tail flaps of an airplane. When a flying squirrel has nearly completed a glide and is about to alight on a tree trunk the tail is suddenly raised. This elevates the plane of the body so that a head-on collision is avoided and the ventral part of the body comes approximately parallel to the vertical landing surface. The glide is their regular mode of progress when travelling through the forest. It is usually started from high in one tree and terminates lower down on the trunk of another tree which may be seventy-five to a hundred feet or more away. Rarely do they descend to the ground except about the bases of larger trees which they will immediately ascend if danger is suspected.

Flying squirrels, like many other kinds of squirrels, tame quite readily. Occasionally, when food is regularly left for them about a camp they will learn to come to it each evening, even overcoming their fear of a lantern or camp fire in time. Their presence at night may sometimes be detected by a soft thud as they land on a nearby tree trunk and a faint scratching as they scramble upward. Occasionally a low chuckle can be heard.

Flying squirrels have relatively large eyes, a character frequently found in nocturnal animals. These squirrels spend the day in holes in living trees and dead snags. These holes generally appear to have been constructed originally by woodpeckers. The cavity occupied by a squirrel is partly filled with bark, needles or other bits of plant material to form a nest.

Little is known of the food of the species in this region but it is likely that it consists largely of the seeds of coniferous trees. It is the experience of most trappers that these animals come readily to meat bait. While trapping for Pine Marten near the Sonora Pass in late November, 1941, I caught 12 flying squirrels in 9 days in steel traps baited with meat and dried fish. Eighteen Red Squirrels were secured in these traps during the same period. If one were to assume that the bait was equally attractive and the traps equally accessible to both kinds of squirrels these figures would indicate 2 flying squirrels to every 3 Red Squirrels in this region which is about 45 miles south of Lake Tahoe.

Flying squirrels, like Red Squirrels, appear to be active all winter. The young, as far as known, are born principally in June and July. The breeding season, however, may be somewhat extended as half-grown young have been found in the central Sierra Nevada as late as the end of October. Records available show the number of young in a litter to vary from 2 to 6.

Practically nothing is known of the natural enemies of these animals but it may be presumed that because of their nocturnal activities they are victims occasionally of some of the larger kinds of owls and perhaps Pine Marten.

FAMILY GEOMYIDAE—Pocket Gophers

MOUNTAIN POCKET GOPHER
Thomomys monticola

Description—Total length, 7½ to 8½ inches; tail length, 2¼ to 3 inches. Body stocky, with the head rather blunt; incisor teeth projecting prominently from the mouth. Cheeks possessing external, fur-lined pouches. Ears, very small. Front legs, larger than hind legs, with long claws present on the feet. Tail, relatively short, stocky and rather scantily haired. Eyes, small. General color above, brown, with small but conspicuous patches of black behind the ears. Fur on feet, tail, and underparts, grayish-white.

General Distribution—The Cascades and the southwestern coastal part of Oregon, south through the higher mountains of northern California and the Sierra Nevada to Fresno County. Occurs in Nevada only in the Lake Tahoe region.

Local Distribution—Of wide occurrence from lake level to timber line. Absent from marshy, densely forested, or very rocky areas.

Habits—Pocket gophers of the genus *Thomomys* are widely distributed over most of western North America, from southern Canada to southern Mexico. Within this extensive area many different kinds occur. Some are inhabitants of the desert, others of valleys, foothills and high mountains. Their blunt, stocky bodies, large, protruding incisor teeth, fur-lined cheek pouches and subterranean habits, however, all combine to make them readily recognizable as pocket gophers, although the differences between the various species are less readily discernible to the amateur.

The Mountain Pocket Gopher, which occurs so commonly in the Lake Tahoe region, is probably better known to most persons by the mounds that it constructs than by actual observations on the living animal. While not as strictly subterranean as moles, pocket gophers have been estimated by some to spend ninety-nine percent of their lives beneath the ground. When they are on the surface, as occasionally occurs when they are after green vegetation, usually only the front part of the body emerges from the burrow opening. One morning when the writer was sitting quietly near the lake shore at the mouth of Ward Creek a pocket gopher was seen to thrust its head out through the mouth of a freshly opened burrow. After remaining motionless at attention for about a quarter of a minute the animal quickly reached out several inches farther and in a matter of a few seconds severed the base of a lupine plant that was 18 inches in height. As soon as the plant was cut off it was pulled to the burrow entrance and bitten in half. Each half in turn was then drawn into the tunnel. Upon returning to this place a little while later the writer noted that the animal had plugged the burrow opening with dirt.

Since nearly all of the activities of pocket gophers are confined to within the walls of their burrows these subterranean passages are extensive and serve a number of purposes. Nest chambers and refuse chambers are provided. Along the course of certain tunnels lateral passageways lead to the surface. Soil that has been excavated beneath the ground with long strong front claws, sometimes aided by strong incisor teeth, is often pushed out through these laterals to the surface where mounds are formed. Much excavated soil, however, is merely pushed into unused tunnels. Since the short laterals do not rise vertically the opening from which the soil has been pushed out generally lies under one side of the mound rather than beneath the center. This is one way of distinguishing pocket gopher "workings" from those of moles. The latter, of course, may also be recognized by the lumpy, rather than pulverized character of the soil composing the mound. Unless burrow entrances are actually in use, such as for excavating or securing surface vegetation, they are kept closed with plugs of earth.

In winter the Mountain Pocket Gopher extends its tunnels above the ground into the overlying snow pack and so is enabled to secure bark and other forms of surface vegetation that are not available during the warmer seasons. Soil is often pushed out into these snow tunnels. When the snow melts in the spring these earthen cores are frequently seen winding over the surface of the ground.

The principal food of pocket gophers consists of roots. In the spring and summer, however, the stems and leaves of many plants supplement this diet. Because of their food habits these animals are serious pests to agriculturists and even home gardeners in certain regions. They are, however, important factors in natural cultivation since they bring subsurface soil to the top and also, by means of their tunnels, aerate the earth.

Pocket gophers are usually solitary animals. It is only during the breeding season that one may occasionally find a male and female in the same burrow. The reproductive season for the species in the central Sierra Nevada is fairly long, extending from May at least to August. Half-grown young have been taken in late June and pregnant females in July. From these data it appears likely that many females bear 2 litters each summer. The number in a litter is known to vary from 3 to 7.

Pocket gophers are most active in the morning and late afternoon. The fact, however, that their remains are often found in the regurgitated pellets of the larger owls indicates that they are active to some extent at night. Weasels are an important enemy of these animals and are frequently captured in pocket gopher burrows. When weasels become established in a locality there is often a noticeable decline in the nearby pocket gopher population. No doubt many other carnivores as well as several kinds of snakes also prey upon these small ground-dwelling rodents.

FAMILY MURIDAE—Rats and Mice

WHITE-FOOTED MICE

DEER MOUSE
Peromyscus maniculatus

Description—Total length, about 6 to 7 inches; tail length, 2½ to 3 inches. Body, slightly larger than that of a House Mouse. Upper parts, yellowish-brown and underparts white. Ears, averaging a little more than one-half an inch in length. Tail, well covered with short hairs, sharply bicolored, dark brown above and white beneath, slightly shorter than combined length of head and body. Fur on feet, distinctly white.

The young of all species of *Peromyscus* in this region are a dark blue-gray above.

General Distribution—From southern Alaska east to Labrador and south to southern Mexico, in general, exclusive of southeastern United States.

Local Distribution—The most abundant and widely distributed mammal in the region.

Brush Mouse
Peromyscus boylii

Description—Total length, 7½ to 8¼ inches; tail length, 3¾ to 4½ inches. The Brush Mouse is most readily distinguished from the Deer Mouse by its larger size and by its tail. The latter is proportionately long, usually exceeding the combined length of the head and body, and rather sparsely haired with the scaly annulations quite evident. This species differs from the True White-footed Mouse in having decidedly smaller ears (about ¾ of an inch in length), a relatively longer, more sparsely haired tail, and shorter body pelage.

General Distribution—From northern California east to Missouri and south to Guatemala.

Local Distribution—Of rare occurrence along the eastern shore of Lake Tahoe.

True White-footed Mouse
Peromyscus truei

Description—Total length, 7 to 8¼ inches; tail length, 3½ to 4 inches. The True White-footed Mouse may be distinguished from either of the two preceding species by its large ears which are about one inch, sometimes slightly more, in length. In body size it is much larger than the Deer Mouse and slightly larger than the Brush Mouse, although the tail is relatively shorter and more heavily haired than in the latter species. The pelage of the True White-footed Mouse is longer and more silky than that of the other two species.

General Distribution—From west-central Oregon east to Colorado and south to southern Mexico.

Local Distribution—Rare in the eastern part of the Lake Tahoe region.

HABITS

Three species of the genus *Peromyscus,* commonly referred to as white-footed mice, have actually been recorded within the Lake Tahoe region. Two of these, the Brush Mouse and the True White-footed Mouse, barely enter the eastern part of the area and, therefore, constitute a relatively insignificant part of its mammalian fauna. The Deer Mouse, however, is without doubt the most abundant mammal about Lake Tahoe or for that matter throughout most of North America.

Few owners of mountain cabins have failed to experience some depredation resulting from the periodic invasions of their domains by these small native rodents. The damage is usually to linens, bedding, curtains or other fabrics, parts of which the mice find appropriate for nest materials, or to various unprotected foods, especially grains and cereals.

Deer Mice range from below sea level, as in Death Valley, California, to above timber line and occur in nearly every kind of available terrestrial habitat to be found within the limits of their range. Because they are strictly nocturnal, do not construct obvious burrows or use well-defined trails, one can rarely gather any impression of the relative numbers of these mice in a region without resorting to trapping. Their homes are usually located in natural crevices in rocks, banks, piles of debris, logs, stumps and the like or in the deserted burrows of other animals. Within the protection of these places they build nests of warm dry materials such as plant fiber or mammal fur.

So far as known there is no evidence to indicate that these mice go into dormancy during the cold season. Even in the high Sierra Nevada in mid-winter their tracks may be seen in the morning if there has been a fresh fall of snow the night before. The food of the Deer Mouse consists principally of the seeds of a wide variety of plants, including grasses, herbs, shrubs, deciduous and coniferous trees. Green vegetation and bark are occasionally eaten, particularly when or where seeds are scarce. Like many other rodents Deer Mice will eat meat at times when it is available, even the bodies of individuals of their own species that have been caught in traps.

The breeding season in the high mountains extends from April or May until September or October. During this time it is probable that adult females produce more than one litter. The number of young in a litter is known to vary from 1 to 9, with the average being between 3 and 4. At time of birth young Deer Mice are blind and naked but within a day or so their juvenile fur begins to make its appearance. This is fully grown by the time they are about a month old so that the upper parts and sides of the head and body present a uniformly gray appearance. Replacement by a more mature type of pelage then commences almost immediately and is completed at the age of about three months. Sexual maturity is attained at an early age by members of this species, judging from the fact that there are records of females only ten weeks old giving birth to young.

The Deer Mouse, because of its abundance, its presence in so many diversified habitats, and its extensive geographic range, has many natural enemies among nocturnal birds, mammals and reptiles. It is an important source of food for many kinds of owls, both small and large, for most of the small and medium-sized carnivores and for several kinds of snakes in this region.

BUSHY-TAILED WOOD RAT
Neotoma cinerea

Description—Total length, 14 to 17 inches; tail length, 5½ to 7 inches. General body form, rat-like, but with fur relatively long and soft. Tail, shorter than combined length of head and body and well-covered with hairs, many of which are over one inch in length. Coloration above, grayish-brown; more grayish on top of tail. Feet and underparts of body and tail, white. Whiskers, long and conspicuous.

General Distribution—From northwestern Canada south throughout most of the mountainous parts of western United States from Washington east to North Dakota and south to the southern Sierra Nevada in California, the mountains of southern Nevada, northern Arizona and northern New Mexico.

Local Distribution—Fairly common wherever rocky crevices or talus slopes are present.

Habits—The Bushy-tailed Wood Rat is the only native species of rat found in the Lake Tahoe region. Its heavily furred, relatively bushy tail serves to distinguish it readily from the several non-native rats that occur in towns and cities at lower elevations as well as from other closely related species of wood rats native to parts of western North America.

Bushy-tailed Wood Rats are widely distributed over the Lake Tahoe region. Droppings and accumulations of sticks and debris belonging to these animals may be found from lake shore to above timber line, wherever there are talus slopes or rocky outcrops.

The terms "pack rat" and "trade rat" are often applied to various kinds of wood rats because of their habit of gathering sticks and other materials. In the course of these meanderings they occasionally come across some bright object of value, such as a spoon, knife or watch. They frequently appropriate these items and it is believed that if they are carrying something else at the time, such as a stick, they drop it in order to take the more attractive object. A one-sided trade thus appears to have been enacted, sometimes to the dismay of a careless camper.

On occasions Bushy-tailed Wood Rats will get into mountain cabins, especially those left unoccupied for some time. These wood rats, however, seldom offer the problems so often presented by their smaller relatives, the Deer Mice. Their usual abode is deep within rocky crevices in which piles of sticks and other materials may or may not be evident to an observer. Hollow logs also serve at times as homes for wood rats. The immediate vicinity of occupied nests is usually characterized by a musky odor which is produced by a glandular secretion from these animals.

The food of Bushy-tailed Wood Rats appears to consist largely of the fruits, nuts or berries of a wide variety of available plants. Occasionally, when food is scarce, they may resort to eating bark. Members of this species are generally quite nocturnal and, as far as known, are active throughout the winter.

In the higher Sierra Nevada most of the young are born in July. The number in a litter varies from 3 to 5 with 4 being about average. The rate of growth of the young is apparently rather rapid as many half-grown individuals are to be found by August.

Not much is known concerning the enemies of Bushy-tailed Wood Rats. It is likely, however, on account of their size and nocturnal habits that they are occasionally captured by larger species of owls as well as various carnivorous mammals, especially weasels and, at higher elevations, Pine Marten.

VOLES

GRAY LEMMING MOUSE
Phenacomys intermedius

Description—Total length, 5½ to 6¼ inches; tail length, 1⅛ to 1½ inches. Body, moderately stocky and relatively long-haired. Resembling a small type of meadow mouse with a proportionately short tail. General color above, pale grayish-brown; underparts whitish. Ears of moderate size (averaging slightly more than one-half inch in length) but largely covered by the fur of the head.

General Distribution—From northern British Columbia and southwestern Alberta south in the Rocky Mountains to Colorado and in the Cascades and Sierra Nevada south at least to Yosemite National Park in California. Not recorded from Nevada.

Local Distribution—Extremely rare, known only from Pyramid Peak and Echo.

MONTANE MEADOW MOUSE
Microtus montanus

Description—Total length, 6 to 7½ inches; tail length, 1½ to 2 inches. Like most voles the Montane Meadow Mouse possesses a stocky body, a blunt nose, relatively long, loose fur, a proportionately short tail, and moderate-sized ears which are largely covered by the long fur on the head. This species is considerably larger and darker than the Gray Lemming Mouse with which it is not likely to be confused. It much more closely resembles the Long-tailed Meadow Mouse from which it may generally be distinguished by its smaller size, shorter tail (usually less than thirty per cent of total length), and darker grayish-brown color.

General Distribution—From southern British Columbia south, in suitable localities, to the southern Sierra Nevada in California and east to New Mexico.

Local Distribution—Usually common in grassy meadows and along the margins of marshes.

P&G MATTSON

LONG-TAILED MEADOW MOUSE
Microtus longicaudus

Description—Total length, 6¾ to 8 inches; tail length, 2¼ to 3 inches. Members of this species are usually distinguishable from Montane Meadow Mice by their larger size, longer tail (usually more than thirty per cent of total length), and lighter, grayish-brown color.

General Distribution—From southeastern Alaska south, in suitable localities, to the San Bernardino Mountains of southern California and east to New Mexico.

Local Distribution—Most abundant along streamsides but occasionally found in meadows and even in dry, brush-covered areas.

HABITS

As is true of a good many members of this group the three species of voles or meadow mouse-like rodents occurring in the Lake Tahoe region differ from each other more as regards their habits than they do in superficial appearances.

The Gray Lemming Mouse is so rare that few persons reading this account are likely to have the opportunity of seeing it in life. In the course of studying and trapping small mammals over a good many years I have never yet seen one of these animals in the Sierra Nevada, although I have had the good luck to capture several in the northern Rocky Mountains. This species, at least in California, occurs near timber line where individuals inhabit small burrows, usually in or close to patches of heather. Very little is known regarding their behavior but it appears that, like many voles, they are occasionally active in the daytime and do not hibernate in winter. A female, collected on July 23, 1932, in northern Idaho, contained four embryos.

Unlike the Gray Lemming Mouse, the Montane and Long-tailed meadow mice are both of common and widespread occurrence about Lake Tahoe. Montane Meadow Mice are restricted to grassy areas where their presence is made known by numerous burrow openings with narrow but sharply marked trails radiating from them. These paths are often partly concealed by overhanging grass stems so as to resemble miniature tunnels or arch ways. Small oblong droppings from the mice and cut bits of grass are generally scattered along their course. These runways made by meadow mice are, as trapping has repeatedly shown, frequently used by other kinds of mammals, such as shrews, white-footed mice, and, on occasion, by their enemies the weasels.

Meadow mice of this species are often active during the day-light hours, especially in the morning. They are likewise active throughout the winter and excavate tunnels in the snow. Sometimes winter nests of dry grass are constructed in these snow tunnels and are evident above ground in spring when the snow has melted and the mice have moved back into the ground.

The food of members of this species consists principally of grass although on occasion they may be forced to resort to other types of vegetable matter including even bark. The breeding season is long, extending from May to October. During this time most adult females probably bear at least two litters of young. The young grow rapidly and often attain sexual maturity within a few weeks. Females less than half-grown have sometimes been found pregnant. The number of young in a litter is usually 6 or 7 with extremes of 4 and 9 known. As can be seen from the foregoing facts the reproductive potential of this species is very high. This perhaps explains why, under certain conditions, outbreaks of these animals occur, especially if some of their natural population checks such as disease or predators fail to function adequately for a short while.

The Long-tailed Meadow Mouse, unlike the preceding species, rarely occurs in open grassland or in marshes. Members of this species are most frequently found living beneath streamside vegetation and occasionally are even found in dry brush. Well-marked trails are not usually in evidence. Furthermore, they are much more strictly nocturnal than are the Montane Meadow Mice. Like that of the latter their breeding season is long and young of the year seem capable of reproducing when several months old. The average number of young in a litter in the central Sierra Nevada appears to be about 5.

Both of the common species of voles in the Lake Tahoe region are important as food for several kinds of hawks, owls and snakes as well as a good many species of carnivorous mammals. These natural enemies of meadow mice would therefore seem to be of considerable importance in preventing abnormal population increases among these small rodents.

MUSKRAT
Ondatra zibethica

Description—Total length, 20 to 24 inches; tail length, about 8 to 10 inches. General appearance, somewhat rat-like with a blunt vole-like nose. Tail, relatively naked, scaly and laterally compressed so as to appear rudder-like. Hind feet, decidedly larger than forefeet, partly webbed, and with a noticeable fringe of hair on the sides of the toes. General color, dark brown.

General Distribution—From Alaska east to Newfoundland and south to northern Mexico.

Local Distribution—Known to occur in the Truckee and Upper Truckee rivers. Recorded from Glenbrook.

Habits—The Muskrat is closely related to meadow mice and is the only truly aquatic rodent in the Lake Tahoe region. The fur of this animal is of considerable commercial value and, in parts of the United States, Muskrat farming and trapping is an important industry. Most of the pelts are processed and sold under the trade name of Hudson Seal. These animals are not sufficiently numerous in the Tahoe area, however, to make trapping worthwhile.

A few Muskrats occur along the Truckee River and also the lower part of the Upper Truckee River. Occasional reports are heard of their occurrence elsewhere, such as near the mouth of Burton Creek and at Glenbrook.

These animals do not construct houses like their eastern relatives. Instead, they live in holes along the banks of water courses. The entrances to these burrows are usually situated below the level of the stream, thus affording the occupants protection from their enemies. Muskrats often build several different types of burrows. Some are used as retreats in which food may be eaten in safety. Others serve as shelters in which the animals sleep. Such burrows usually have a nest chamber which is lined with dry vegetation. Breeding dens where the young are born and cared for are generally more complicated than those used for eating or sleeping. These burrows often have more than the usual two entrances and are characterized by a number of complicated communicating passageways.

Muskrats are occasionally observed in the daytime or early evening but, for the most part, they are active at night. Their footprints and the tracks left by their long tails may often be seen in the mud along the shores of the streams previously mentioned. Since the stems of tules and cat-tails provide the principal food for Muskrats the presence of such plants is probably an important factor influencing the distribution of these animals.

Little is known concerning the breeding habits of this species in the Sierra Nevada. Along the lower Colorado River, according to Grinnell, Dixon and Linsdale (1937), young are produced every month in the year. In the Tahoe region, however, it is likely that the females bear young only during the late spring and summer months. The number of young in a litter in many localities is said to average about six.

Large hawks and owls as well as Coyotes and Raccoons are the principal natural enemies of Muskrats.

FAMILY APLODONTIIDAE—Mountain Beaver

MOUNTAIN BEAVER
Aplodontia rufa

Description—Total length, 12 to 14 inches; tail length, averaging slightly over 1 inch. Body, stocky and fairly large for a rodent, larger than a ground squirrel and smaller than a marmot. Tail, so small as to be almost indistinguishable in life. Eyes and ears, both relatively small. Legs, rather short and claws adapted for digging. Fur, of medium length and rather coarse. Color, dark grayish-brown above, somewhat lighter beneath. Whiskers moderately long and conspicuous.

General Distribution—The Pacific slope of western North America, from southern British Columbia south along the coast to Marin County, California; in the Sierra Nevada, south to the vicinity of Sequoia National Park; entering Nevada only in the Lake Tahoe region.

Local Distribution—Fairly common near small streams and rivulets, particularly where dense growths of mountain alder, thimbleberry and bracken fern are present.

Habits—The Mountain Beaver or Sewellel is not a close relative of the true Beaver, apart from the fact that they are both rodents. Indeed, it is the only living species of its family and occurs nowhere else in the world, other than in western North America. Few persons have occasion to see this interesting animal because of its natural shyness, nocturnal prediliction and preference for dense plant cover.

Mountain Beavers are fairly common, locally, along the lower courses of the smaller streams flowing into Lake Tahoe from the west, and have also been found along Incline Creek and at Marlette Lake to the north and east, respectively. Their extensive systems of tunnels and runways, as well as burrow entrances, are most frequently found if one searches beneath dense streamside vegetation. The tunnels are usually from 2 to 10 feet in length and are situated close to the surface of the ground. They alternate regularly with exposed surface runways and often, in the early summer, water from nearby streams and seepages is diverted into them. Sometimes several of the tunnel-runway systems will be seen to converge at the entrance to a deep underground burrow. The burrows and tunnels are of fairly large diameter, usually measuring from 6 to 10 inches across.

The food of the Mountain Beaver consists of the leaves and bark of a good many kinds of herbaceous plants, shrubs and small trees. The author has found that members of this species consumed columbine, creek dogwood, alder, willow, bracken fern, fat solomon, fairy bells and several kinds of grasses. While most of the food plants are secured on the ground, Mountain Beavers will occasionally climb a short distance up into small trees, such as mountain alders, in foraging. On August 17, 1938, near Eagle Falls, an individual of this species was observed by the author to ascend the sloping trunk of an alder, to a distance of about 6 feet above the ground. After climbing to this height it proceeded to cut off a branch about 2½ feet long and ½ an inch in diameter, carry it to the ground in its mouth and drag it into a tangled growth of thimbleberry. Such branches are generally cut for the purpose of securing bark.

In the late summer and early autumn Mountain Beavers have the curious habit of building "hay piles." These are piles of freshly cut vegetation that are stacked and left for a few days to dry. Sometimes they may attain a height of several feet. Whether this dried vegetation is stored for winter use as food, or whether it is for nest material is not definitely known. These piles are usually placed close to the entrance to a tunnel or burrow into which they are taken when "cured."

Mountain Beavers are active all winter. At this season of the year they burrow extensively beneath the snow and feed principally on bark. These animals are generally quite silent but occasionally can be heard emitting a grunting sound. If injured they are capable of making a rather shrill cry which can be heard for quite a few yards. In captivity they are surly and show little inclination to become tame. Under such circumstances they spend most of their active hours trying to gnaw their way to freedom and generally are successful within a remarkably short time, unless their cage is composed entirely of metal.

Although Mountain Beavers seem to occur commonly in certain localities and be absent from other seemingly suitable situations they are in no sense colonial. The young, 2 or 3 in number, are born in the spring. It seems unlikely that the female bears more than one litter annually.

Little is known regarding the natural enemies of Mountain Beavers. However, as these animals are fairly large in size, possess powerful jaws and teeth capable of inflicting serious injury on an opponent, and rarely venture far from their burrows, it is likely that they do not have many bird or mammal enemies.

FAMILY ZAPODIDAE—Jumping Mice

P & G MATTSON

BIG JUMPING MOUSE
Zapus princeps

Description—Total length, 8½ to 9½ inches; tail length, 5 to 6 inches. Fur, rather coarse and stiff. Hairs on top of head and back, blackish with a small amount of orange-brown evident. Sides of head and body and front of legs, bright orange-brown with only a sprinkling of black present. Fur on underparts, pure white in marked contrast to the upper parts of the body. Ears, proportionately small for a mouse. Hind feet, long in contrast with forefeet. Tail, nearly naked, with pronounced scaly rings, and generally more than one and one-half times the combined length of the head and body.

General Distribution—From northern British Columbia and western Saskatchewan south to Sequoia National Park in the Sierra Nevada of California and east to New Mexico.

Local Distribution—Most frequently found along the margins of streams and rivulets where there is a lush growth of herbaceous vegetation, or about the margins of wet meadows.

Habits—The jumping mice of the mountains, like the kangaroo rats and pocket mice that are so common in the lowlands and deserts of the West, possess relatively large hind legs and feet which enable them to bound 2 or 3 feet at a time. Their long tails serve as balancing organs when they are so leaping. Several kinds of jumping mice occur in North America and Asia but, as far as known, this species is the largest.

The Big Jumping Mouse is an inhabitant of damp places near streams and about the margins of wet meadows, especially where there is an abundance of grass and a luxuriant growth of herbaceous plants. These animals, at least during the warmer months of the year, live in globular grass nests that are inconspicuously situated on the surface of the ground. The vegetation used in constructing such a nest is usually dry grass of the previous year.

Jumping mice are largely nocturnal, but in areas where they are abundant one will occasionally arouse them from their nests in the daytime. Under such circumstances their rather bright and contrasting coloration makes them quite conspicuous. Their presence may sometimes be detected by the appearance of freshly cut plant stems on the ground. These cuttings are longer than those of meadow mice, generally being 1 to 2 inches in length. Judging from the observations of others jumping mice may occasionally take to water and can swim quite well.

The food of members of this species consists principally of the stems, leaves and seeds of a number of kinds of grasses and herbs. In the late summer these animals become very fat in preparation for their long winter sleep. Hibernation apparently begins early as it is unusual to find jumping mice active after September. It is probable that the period of dormancy is passed in underground burrows or in nests beneath logs, tree roots or other solid objects where there would be greater security than that afforded by their summer homes in the grass. Little is known, however, regarding this phase of their life history.

The young are born early in the summer. The number in a litter is fairly high, in many localities averaging about 6. The enemies of jumping mice in the Tahoe area are probably the same as those of other small, nocturnal, ground-dwelling rodents.

FAMILY ERETHIZONTIDAE—Porcupines

P & G MATTSON

NORTH AMERICAN PORCUPINE
Erethizon dorsatum

Description—Total length, 27 to 32 inches; tail length, 7 to 9 inches. The large size, blunt nose and long, yellow-tipped hairs, combined with the presence of an abundance of yellowish-white quills that are tipped with black, on the upper parts and sides of the head, body, and tail serve to identify members of this species.

General Distribution—From Alaska east to Labrador and south, in western United States, to New Mexico.

Local Distribution—Fairly common throughout the Tahoe region, especially where there are coniferous forests close to rocky outcrops.

Habits—Nature has equipped porcupines with such a formidable defense mechanism in the form of sharply pointed quills that
they have relatively little to fear from most of their would-be
enemies. They are slow on foot and show little desire to fight in
self-defense. If danger threatens they merely curl their head under
the front part of the body and raise their quills so as to present
the appearance of a living pincushion. If approached closely the
bristling tail is lashed. Unfortunate indeed is the animal or human
who contacts this weapon. The quills themselves are stiff and finely
barbed at their tips. Furthermore, they are very easily detached
from the porcupine's skin. Inexperienced dogs, Coyotes and even
Bobcats sometimes find this out too late.

Porcupines are fairly common throughout the Tahoe region
and, because they are sometimes active in the daytime, are occasionally seen by visitors. They frequently make their homes in
dens in rocks. Numerous oval or slightly curved droppings, about
an inch in length and composed of wood pulp, are evidence of
of their presence. It is reported that in winter a dozen or more
individuals may occupy a single den.

Porcupines are primarily forest dwellers, although they are not
necessarily restricted to such a habitat. On occasions I have seen
them out on the Nevada deserts many miles from trees. Their
principal food in the Sierra Nevada consists of the soft, growing
layer of trees, just beneath the bark. Although willow, service
berry, desert mahogany and many other non-coniferous trees and
shrubs may be eaten they show definite preference for the bark of
pines such as lodgepole, Jeffrey and sugar pine. Red and white fir
are somewhat less desirable. Lumbermen are often resentful of
porcupines because of the latter's preference for pines, especially
those of commercial value. Porcupines, however, are the natural
pruners of the forest. Locally they may do damage but this is
usually in areas where man has already removed the choicest timber for his own purposes. Vast forests inhabited by porcupines

thrived and attained perfection in North America long before man made his appearance.

In defense of the porcupine it may be said that it has a fondness for mistletoe as a food. Since members of the mistletoe family are parasitic, some living on deciduous trees, and others on conifers, they tend to devitalize their hosts. Trees so affected may sometimes die as a direct result of heavy mistletoe infestation, or indirectly by becoming so weakened that they succumb to some disease. Consequently, porcupines by destroying quantities of this parasite may be of considerable benefit to a forest. Although the flesh of the porcupine offers no great treat to the epicure, it is, nevertheless, edible. Since the animals themselves are slow-moving and can be secured with no more formidable a weapon than a club, woodsmen have long regarded them as a valuable source of food to one lost in the wilds.

The reproductive rate of porcupines is relatively low. Perhaps this is because these animals are long-lived and have very few enemies. Generally the adult females bear one young each summer. The young at birth are well covered with long hair, have their eyes open and are capable of running about actively within a few hours. Some observers have noted short quills on the body at this time while in other instances it would appear that they do not begin to protrude through the skin for several days. The mother porcupine pays little attention to her young and the latter is on its own after about one week of nursing. Young porcupines are reported to be very wary in contrast to the indifferent adults. This is probably an adaptation to increase their chances of attaining maturity in view of the absence of parental protection.

Mention has already been made of the occasional attacks on porcupines by Coyotes and Bobcats. The Fisher is considered by many to be the only major enemy with which these animals have to contend. This carnivore, however, is now so reduced in numbers throughout most of its range that is can hardly be of significance at present in reducing the porcupine population.

ORDER LAGOMORPHA—Rabbit-like Mammals
FAMILY OCHOTONIDAE—Pikas

PIKA
Ochotona princeps

Description—Total length, 6¾ to 8 inches; tail, so small that it is hardly discernible on the living animal. General color of back and sides, grayish-brown. Top and sides of head, gray. Underparts, buffy. Fur, relatively long, soft and rabbit-like. Ears, rounded and about 1 inch in length. Soles of front and hind feet furred, except for naked toe pads.

General Distribution—From British Columbia and Alberta south to the southern Sierra Nevada in California and east to the mountains of northern New Mexico.

Local Distribution—Fairly common in the Tahoe region but limited to rock slides largely above the 7500-foot level.

Habits—The Pika or Cony is probably one of the lesser known mammals of the Lake Tahoe region. There is no reason, however, why anyone with a little patience should not become familiar with these interesting little relatives of the rabbits. Wherever there are extensive rock slides in the higher Sierra Nevada there are usually Pikas.

No doubt many persons on the way to Mt. Tallac, the Velma Lakes or on the slopes of Mt. Rose, Ward Peak, even on the talus slopes above Eagle Falls, have heard the calls of these little animals without being aware of the identity of the maker. The call notes might best be described as a fairly loud nasal bleat uttered two or three times in rapid succession. Careful observation of the rock slide from which the sounds seem to emanate will often reveal a small, hunched-up bundle of fur perched motionless on a boulder far up the slope, acting as a sentinel. If the observer remains quiet fear may be dispelled and other Pikas inhabiting the slide may resume some of their regular daily activities. The presence of Pikas on a talus slope can usually be determined quite quickly by the abundant droppings which these animals deposit on the rocks. These droppings look like small round pellets and frequently are concentrated about their observation posts.

Pikas are strictly diurnal and do not come out until the sun has been up for several hours, dispelling the chill of the previous night. They, likewise, disappear in the late afternoon. Their calls, however, may be heard after these hours from deep in their rocky homes if one disturbs them. This is also true in winter when they may be heard below the heavy mantle of snow which often imprisons them for long periods of time.

Pikas feed on a number of kinds of plants that grow along the margins of talus slopes. Their food varies, therefore, to a considerable extent with locality. In the late summer and early autumn of 1935 I regularly watched a group of Pikas harvesting vegetation for use as winter food on a slope above Emerald Bay. "Hay piles," containing as much as one cubic yard of leaves, were found in rock crevices under large overhanging boulders. The plants selected as food to be stored until winter, as well as those eaten daily, were bitter cherry, huckleberry oak, snow brush and bracken fern. Tougher species such as green manzanita and pine-mat manzanita, both of which were growing nearby in abundance, were left untouched.

Pikas, because of their restriction largely to talus slopes, are often associated with other rock-frequenting types of mammals such as Golden-mantled Ground Squirrels, California Ground Squirrels, several kinds of chipmunks, Bushy-tailed Woodrats and their most deadly enemies the weasels and Pine Marten.

The reproductive season for members of this species is fairly extensive, young being born any time from May to September, inclusive. The usual number in a litter is 3 or 4. By the time they are one-third grown they can be seen running about over the rocks like the adults.

FAMILY LEPORIDAE—Hares and Rabbits

WHITE-TAILED JACK RABBIT
Lepus townsendii

Description—Total length, 22 to 26 inches; tail length, 2½ to 4¼ inches. A large, heavy-bodied jack rabbit that is grayish-brown in summer pelage and white in winter pelage. Distinguishable at all seasons of the year from the Black-tailed Jack Rabbit by its conspicuous white tail. Differs from the Snowshoe Rabbit by its much greater size and preference for open or semi-open country rather than forests.

General Distribution—The mountains and plains of western North America from southern Canada south to Missouri on the east and to the higher southern Sierra Nevada in California on the west.

Local Distribution—Relatively rare in the Lake Tahoe region. Confined principally, at least during the summer months, to the higher peaks, close to or above timber line. In winter, frequently found at lower levels.

SNOWSHOE RABBIT
Lepus americanus

Description—Total length, 14 to 17 inches; tail length, 1 to
1½ inches. General color of upper parts in summer pelage, cin-
namon-brown. Margins of ears and tops of front and hind feet,
white. Tail, rather inconspicuous, brownish above, dusky beneath.
Color in winter pelage, white.

General Distribution—From northern Alaska east to Newfoundland and south to northern United States except in the West
where the range of the species extends south in the Rocky Mountains to New Mexico and in the Sierra Nevada to Tuolumne
County, California.

Local Distribution—Not uncommon, even at lake level, especially where there is an abundance of dense streamside vegetation,
forest undergrowth, or conifer thickets.

BLACK-TAILED JACK RABBIT
Lepus californicus

Description—Total length, 20 to 23 inches; tail length, 2½
to 4 inches. Lighter in build than the White-tailed Jack Rabbit

with general color of upper parts buffy-gray at all seasons of the year. Top of tail always conspicuously black; underside dusky.

General Distribution—Western North America from south-eastern Washington east to Missouri, south to the tip of Baja California and south-central Mexico. Widely distributed over much of California and Nevada.

Local Distribution—The Tahoe region in general is too high for members of this species. Individuals which probably wander in from the lower country to the eastward are occasionally seen.

HABITS

The hares, as a group, are distinguished from the true rabbits by a number of characters. As a general rule they are decidedly larger. Perhaps the most striking difference between the two is the appearance of the young at time of birth. Newborn rabbits are helpless creatures, naked or essentially so, and are blind. Newborn hares, on the other hand, are well furred, have their eyes open and can hop about within a short time. Three distinct species of hares are known to occur in the Lake Tahoe region. The term rabbit, however, used in a loose sense, is associated with the name of each.

The White-tailed Jack Rabbit is a large, heavy-bodied animal that occurs, locally, from the crest of the Sierra Nevada, eastward to the Great Plains of the Mississippi Valley. In the Lake Tahoe region it may be classified as rare and an inhabitant of exposed, flat-topped ridges above 8500 feet during the warmer parts of the year. These big hares are largely nocturnal. During the daytime they generally remain well hidden beneath the dense foliage of prostrate, wind-swept conifers, such as lodgepole and white-bark pines. It is only by accident that one, on a rare occasion, may dislodge a resting individual. There is a likelihood that in winter some of these animals migrate to lower levels.

The Black-tailed Jack Rabbit, which is often so abundant on the Nevada deserts or in the valleys of California, is of rare occurrence in this region. Somewhat smaller and lighter bodied than the White-tailed Jack Rabbit this animal is more at home in lower, open or brush-covered land. The few Black-tails that are seen about Tahoe are probably wanderers from the east.

The commonest hare in the Lake Tahoe region is the Snowshoe Rabbit or Varying Hare. The latter name is widely used for members of this species because of their variable color. Throughout most of the range of the species individuals acquire a white coat in winter that is replaced in summer by one that is brown. This is an adaptive character shared with the White-tailed Jack Rabbit as well as the two kinds of weasels in the Lake Tahoe region. In a snow-covered environment white winter fur is as advantageous to a defenseless animal, like a hare, as it is to a hunter, such as the weasel. The former is less liable to be detected by its enemies while the latter is less conspicuous when approaching a prospective victim. The dense matting of hair on the soles of the hind feet serves to keep these animals from sinking deeply in the snow and is responsible for the name "snowshoe."

The Snowshoe Rabbit is one of the few forest-dwelling hares. During the daylight hours members of this species rest beneath the cover of dense forest undergrowth, streamside vegetation, or in conifer thickets. Like most hares and rabbits they are abroad in the evening and early morning as well as during parts of the night. At such times they are occasionally seen in forests, small clearings, or along the margins of meadows close to cover. They feed on a wide variety of plants, including grasses, herbs, shrubs and, in winter when food is scarce, even the bark of certain deciduous trees.

Like most other hares the Snowshoe Rabbit avoids burrows. As far as known the females fail to construct a nest of any sort for the young when they are born. In this respect they differ from the jack rabbits, the females of which generally provide a shallow cavity lined with fur from their own bodies. The number of young Snowshoe Rabbits in a litter may vary from 1 to 6, although the usual number is 4 or 5. The babies are hidden beneath brush or some sort of cover and do not venture out on their own for some days after birth. By the time they are two weeks old, however, they begin to forage for themselves.

Because hares are of fair size and are frequently active in the open by daylight as well as after dark they have many natural enemies among the carnivorous mammals and birds. Coyotes, Bobcats, Horned Owls, several species of larger hawks, and Golden Eagles are their principal foes in many localities. The young of course fall helpless victims to many smaller predaceous birds and mammals as well as certain snakes.

NUTTALL COTTONTAIL

Sylvilagus nuttallii

Description—Total length, 13½ to 15½ inches; tail length, 1½ to 2 inches. Decidedly smaller than any of the hares or than the domesticated rabbit. General color above, grayish. Underparts of body, white except for chest which is like back. Tail, proportionately large and conspicuously white on underside. Fronts of fore- and hind legs, rusty-orange, this color sometimes extending partly down on the otherwise white tops of the hind feet.

General Distribution—The higher, arid parts of western North America from eastern Washington east to southern Saskatchewan and south to eastern California, southern Nevada, Arizona and New Mexico.

Local Distribution—Present in small numbers in the eastern part of the Lake Tahoe region, especially in rocky, sagebrush-covered areas.

Habits—The Nuttall Cottontail is principally a Great Basin and Rocky Mountain species whose range extends westward as far as the eastern base of the Sierra Nevada. Throughout much of Nevada and parts of eastern California these rabbits are found living on rocky, sage-covered hills and canyons or along streams and rivers where they are afforded protection by dense clumps of willows or other kinds of riparian vegetation.

Like other kinds of cottontails members of this species are most active in the early morning and evening hours. In many localities their principal food throughout the year consists of the leaves and stems of sagebrush. Other plants, especially grasses, are also eaten.

Nuttall Cottontails sometimes inhabit burrows but more commonly they spend their resting hours in rock piles or merely under the cover of dense vegetation, usually of a brushy type. During their hours of activity they seldom venture far into the open. At the first sign of danger they generally dash to the edge of nearby brush and, if further alarmed, disappear behind this protective vegetation. Their course under such circumstances is rarely direct to any hiding place but rather a circuitous one to mislead the pursuer. Unlike jack rabbits cottontails are not built for running long distances to elude their enemies.

Like other rabbits and hares these cottontails are active in winter as well as summer. Their long, dense coat of gray fur serves to protect them against the severe cold of their winter environment and, likewise, harmonizes with the color of the surrounding vegetation.

The blind and essentially naked young are born in the spring and early summer months. The first two weeks or so of their lives are spent in a soft, warm nest which the mother constructs and lines with fur plucked from her own body. These nests are generally situated in a depression in the ground and so camouflaged by the female with dry grass, sticks or other debris that it is only by accident that one discovers them. The number of young in a litter may vary from at least 4 to 8, although the average number is about 6.

Nuttall Cottontails have many enemies, including Coyotes, Bobcats, Horned Owls, Golden Eagles, Red-tailed Hawks, Marsh Hawks and even rattlesnakes.

ORDER ARTIODACTYLA—Even-toed Hoofed Mammals

FAMILY CERVIDAE—Deer, Elk, etc.

MULE AND BLACK-TAILED DEER
Odocoileus hemionus

Description—Total length, varying from about 4 feet 8 inches to 5 feet 8 inches in full-grown adults. Large-bodied, slender-legged, even-toed, hoofed mammals. General color above, yellowish-brown in summer, and grayish-brown in winter. Males possessing dichotomously forked antlers which are grown anew each year. (For the differences between Mule Deer and Black-tailed Deer see *Habits*.)

General Distribution—Western North America from southeastern Alaska, south to northern Mexico and east to the Great Plains of the Mississippi Valley.

Local Distribution—Widely distributed over most of the Tahoe region, from lake level to timber line. Less numerous during the winter season.

Habits—For many years the Black-tailed Deer which occurs on the Pacific coast, west of the main Sierra Nevada-Cascade crest, was considered as a species distinct from the Mule Deer that occurs immediately to the eastward. Along the slopes of these mountains, however, there is a definite seasonal movement of the deer populations. In summer some of the Black-tails move up and over the summit onto the eastern side, while a certain proportion of the Mule Deer move in the opposite direction onto the western slopes. As a consequence, during part of the year, there are extensive areas occupied in common by both kinds of deer. Lake Tahoe is such a region.

In the fall, before the breeding season begins, there is generally a return migration so that the two types are separated at the critical rutting period. Along the main Sierra Nevada-Cascade axis, however, there are several low spots where relatively mild winter conditions prevail. In these regions a certain proportion of the Black-tailed Deer and Mule Deer fail to migrate to the westward and eastward, respectively, in the autumn. Furthermore, these populations hybridize freely and produce fertile offspring of an intermediate character. This has led many mammalogists in recent years to consider these two kinds of deer as members of the same species.

Throughout this book I have purposely refrained from any consideration of the subspecies involved in the case of geographically variable mammals. Such problems, generally, are of interest only to the specialist and have no place in a work such as this. In the present instance, however, exception had to be made because of the distinctness of the two kinds of deer that are present together during the summer season in parts of the Lake Tahoe region and because so many sportsmen and other lovers of the out-of-doors are aware of these differences.

For the benefit of those not familiar with Black-tailed and Mule Deer the best characters for distinguishing them in this area, apart from the larger size and larger ears of the latter, are based upon the color of the tail and the length of the metatarsal gland. The Black-tailed Deer, as the name implies, has the dorsal or upper surface of the tail black from the base to the tip. In these animals the metatarsal gland, which is located on the leg between the hock and the hoof, is rarely more than a fraction over 3 inches in length. In the Mule Deer, in general, the upper side of the tail is white at the base so that the black is confined to the terminal half of the dorsal surface. The metatarsal gland in this form averages about 5 inches in length.

Both of these kinds of deer are inhabitants of open forest and brushland. Small mountain meadows are especially attractive to them during the spring and summer months when there is an abundance of green grass. It must not be inferred, however, that deer are primarily grasseaters. They do graze to some extent, but for the most part they are browsing animals, most of their food consisting of the leaves and stems of a wide variety of shrubs. A few of the more important food plants for deer in the Lake Tahoe region are snow brush, huckleberry oak, service berry, bitter cherry, mountain mahogany and green manzanita. Where food is scarce, especially in the fall and winter, the needles and terminal twigs of coniferous trees are occasionally eaten.

Deer are most active in the early morning and evening hours. During the remainder of the day they generally bed down in protected situations in thickets or beneath trees. Such resting places are usually so situated, however, that the occupant is able to detect the approach of danger, either by sight or smell. As most deer hunters know the older and perhaps wiser bucks frequently bed near the tops of the higher ridges so that they have an unobstructed view of the surrounding country.

Deer may walk or run when moderately disturbed but their most spectacular gait is to be seen when they are fully alarmed. Under these last circumstances they take off, usually up a slope, in great leaps and bounds which are quite capable of carrying them over the tops of the brush.

In this region the young are born in June and July. While most does have a single fawn about one out of four have twins. The young at birth are spotted and retain these spots, even though they finally become very faint, for about four months or until they acquire a new coat in the fall. The fawns are weaned when they are 8 to 10 weeks old, although they may follow the mother right through the winter subsequent to their birth, sometimes even longer.

There is no question but that the Mountain Lion is the chief natural enemy of deer. These large native cats have been so reduced in numbers during the past several generations, however, that they presently play an insignificant rôle in controlling deer populations. The white man is now the principal agent responsible for reducing the numbers of deer. A few are killed each year by Coyotes and Bobcats, especially the fawns in the winter when there is deep snow. Golden Eagles are also reported to have captured spotted fawns.

GLOSSARY

aërial. Of or pertaining to the air.

annulations. Rings.

arboreal. Inhabiting or frequenting trees.

bicolored. Of two colors.

canine teeth. The pointed teeth between the incisors and the premolars. In the upper jaw, the eye teeth.

carnivorous. Flesh-eating.

chaparral. A collective term applied to dense growths of rigid or thorny shrubs.

color phase. One of two or more types of coloration.

conifer. Cone-bearing trees and shrubs such as the pines, firs and junipers.

crepuscular. Active in the twilight.

cusp. A prominence or point, particularly on the crown of a tooth.

dappled. Variegated or spotted.

diastema. Refers particularly to the space or gap between the incisor and premolar teeth in rodents.

distal. Remote or away from the point of reference or attachment.

dichotomous. Repeatedly branched or bifurcated.

diurnal. Active in the daytime.

dorsal. Referring to the back or upper parts.

Great Basin. A vast arid plateau of interior drainage, limited on the west by the Sierra Nevada and to the eastward by the Wasatch Mountains of Utah. Includes most of Nevada, western Utah, and parts of southern Idaho, eastern Oregon and northeastern California.

gregarious. Living in groups or colonies.

habitat. The environment in which a plant or animal lives.

herbivorous. Eating or living on plants.

incisors. The front teeth.

insectivorous. Feeding on or consuming insects.

123

litter. A collective term applied to a group of young produced at one time by a single animal.

molariform. Of or pertaining to teeth resembling molars. Often used to include premolars as well as molars when the former bear a resemblance to the latter in form.

nocturnal. Active at night.

omnivorous. Eating both animal and vegetable food.

pelage. The covering or coat of a mammal, such as wool or fur.

pelt. The hide or skin of an animal, most commonly that of a fur-bearing mammal.

premolar. The teeth in front of the molars and behind the canines, if the latter are present.

proximal. Nearest to the point of reference or attachment.

receptor. A receiver.

retractile. Capable of being drawn back or in, as the claws of a cat.

riparian. Of, pertaining to, or living on, the bank of a stream or river; streamside.

rutting period. Breeding season.

subspecies. A geographical race of a species.

tail length. The distance from the base of the tail to the tip, exclusive of the hairs.

talus. Rocky debris accumulated at the base of a cliff or slope; a rock slide.

total length. The distance from the tip of the nose to the end of the tail, exclusive of the hairs.

undulating. Moving back and forth or up and down in waves.

ventral. Of or pertaining to the belly or underside.

vernacular name. The common or native name, as opposed to the technical or scientific name.

LIST OF REFERENCES

ALLEN, GLOVER M.
1939. Bats. Harvard University Press, Cambridge, Massachusetts, pp. x + 368, frontispiece + 57 figs.

ANTHONY, HAROLD E.
1928. Field book of North American mammals. G. P. Putnam's Sons, New York—London, pp. i - xxv + 625, 48 plates, 150 figs., 1 map.

CAHALANE, VICTOR H.
1945. Meeting the mammals. The Macmillan Co., New York, pp. ix + 133, illustrated.
1947. Mammals of North America. The Macmillan Co., New York, pp. x + 682, illustrated.

DIXON, JOSEPH
1934. A study of the life history and food habits of mule deer in California. California Fish and Game, vol. 20, part 1, pp. 181-282, figs. 47-111; part 2, pp. 315-354, figs. 116-135.

GRINNELL, JOSEPH
1933. Review of the recent mammal fauna of California. University of California Publ. Zool., vol. 40, pp. 71-234.

GRINNELL, JOSEPH, and DIXON, JOSEPH
1918. Natural history of the ground squirrels of California. Monthly Bulletin California State Comm. Horticulture [Sacramento, California], vol. 7, pp. 597-708, 5 plates, 30 figs.

GRINNELL, JOSEPH, DIXON, JOSEPH, and LINSDALE, JEAN M.
1930. Vertebrate natural history of a section of northern California through the Lassen Peak region. University of California Publ. Zool., vol. 35, pp. v + 1-594, 181 figs.
1937. Fur-bearing mammals of California: their natural history, systematic status, and relations to man. University of California Press, Berkeley, California, 2 vols., pp. xii + 375 and XIV + 377-777 pp., 13 colored plates, 345 figs.

GRINNELL, JOSEPH, and STORER, TRACY I.
  1924. Animal life in the Yosemite. University of California Press, Berkeley, California, pp. xviii + 752, 62 plates, 65 figs.

HALL, E. RAYMOND
  1946. Mammals of Nevada. University of California Press, Berkeley and Los Angeles, pp. xi + 710, colored frontispiece, 11 plates, 485 figs.

HAMILTON, WILLIAM J., JR.
  1939. American mammals. McGraw-Hill Book Co., Inc., New York and London, pp. xii + 434, frontispiece, 92 figs.

HOWELL, ARTHUR H.
  1915. Revision of the American marmots. U. S. Department of Agriculture, Bureau of Biological Survey, North American Fauna, 37, pp. 1-80, 15 plates, 3 figs.

  1929. Revision of the American chipmunks (genera *Tamias* and *Eutamias*). U. S. Department of Agriculture, Bureau of Biological Survey, North American Fauna, 52, pp. 1-157, 10 plates, 9 figs.

  1938. Revision of the North American ground squirrels with a classification of the North American Sciuridae. U. S. Department of Agriculture, Bureau of Biological Survey, North American Fauna, 56, pp. 1-256, 32 plates, 20 figs.

INGLES, LLOYD G.
  1947. Mammals of California. Stanford University Press, Stanford University, California, pp. xix + 258, 42 plates, 57 figs.

JACKSON, HARTLEY H. T.
  1928. A taxonomic review of the American long-tailed shrews. U. S. Department of Agriculture, Bureau of Biological Survey, North American Fauna, 51, pp. vi + 238, 13 plates, 24 figs.

JAMES, GEORGE WHARTON
  1915. The Lake of the sky, Lake Tahoe. . . . George Wharton James, Pasadena, pp. xiii + 395, illustrated.

LINSDALE, JEAN M.

1946. The California ground squirrel. University of California Press, Berkeley and Los Angeles, pp. xi + 475, 140 figs.

ORR, ROBERT T.

1940. The rabbits of California. Occasional Papers California Academy of Sciences, 19, pp. 1-227, 10 plates, 30 figs.

RENSCH, HERO E., RENSCH, ETHEL G., and HOOVER, MILDRED B.

1933. Historic spots in California: Valley and Sierra Counties. Stanford University Press, Stanford University, California, pp. xxiii + 597.

SETON, ERNEST T.

1909. Life-histories of northern animals. Charles Scribner's Sons, New York City, vol. 1, pp. xxx + 1-673, illustrated; vol. 2, pp. xii + 674-1267, illustrated.

STORER, TRACY I.

1942. Control of injurious rodents in California. California Agricultural Extension Service, Circular 79, pp. 1-66, 29 figs.

:: , v, 1, 4, 10, 15 40, 43, 57 84, 76 - 81, 112, 126

Date Due

P. Wilson		
NOV 2 8 '51		
NOV 2 3 '53		
NOV 1 7 '53		
OCT 9		
OCT 1 0 '56		
JUN 1 '60		
OCT 29 '62		
NOV 5 '62		
NOV 1 9 1970		
MAY 1 1975		
MAY 1 1975		

LIBRARY BUREAU FORM 1137

COM